OXFORD BIBLE SERIES

General editors
P. R. Ackroyd and G. N. Stanton

OXFORD BIBLE SERIES

General editors
P. R. Ackroyd and G. N. Stanton

Wisdom and Law
in the Old Testament

The Ordering of Life
in Israel and Early Judaism

JOSEPH BLENKINSOPP

OXFORD UNIVERSITY PRESS

1995

Oxford University Press, Walton Street, Oxford OX2 6DP

Oxford New York
Athens Auckland Bangkok Bombay
Calcutta Cape Town Dar es Salaam Delhi
Florence Hong Kong Istanbul Karachi
Kuala Lumpur Madras Madrid Melbourne
Mexico City Nairobi Paris Singapore Taipei
Tokyo Toronto
and associated companies in
Berlin Ibadan

Oxford is a trade mark of Oxford University Press

Published in the United States
by Oxford University Press Inc., New York

British Library Cataloguing in Publication Data
Data available

Library of Congress Cataloging in Publication Data
Data available
ISBN 0–19–875503–1
ISBN 0–19–875504–X (Pbk)

1 3 5 7 9 10 8 6 4 2

Set by Hope Services (Abingdon) Ltd.
Printed in Great Britain
on acid-free paper by
Biddles Ltd.
Guildford & King's Lynn

GENERAL EDITORS' PREFACE

There are many commentaries on individual books of the Bible, but the reader who wishes to take a broader view has less choice. This series is intended to meet this need. Its structure is thematic, with each volume embracing a number of biblical books. It is designed for use with any of the familiar translations of the Bible; quotations are normally from RSV, but the authors of the individual volumes also use other translations or make their own where this helps to bring out the particular meaning of a passage.

To provide general orientation, there are two volumes of a more introductory character: one will consider the Old Testament in its cultural and historical context, the other the New Testament, discussing the origins of Christianity. Four volumes deal with different kinds of material in the Old Testament: narrative, prophecy, poetry/psalmody, wisdom and law. Three volumes handle different aspects of the New Testament: the Gospels, Paul and Pauline Christianity, the varieties of New Testament thought. One volume looks at the nature of biblical interpretation, covering both Testaments.

The authors of the individual volumes write for a general readership. Technical terms and Hebrew or Greek words are explained; the latter are used only when essential to the understanding of the text. The general introductory volumes are designed to stand on their own, providing a framework, but also to serve to raise some of the questions which the remaining volumes examine in closer detail. All the volumes other than the two general ones include a discussion of selected biblical passages in greater depth, thus providing examples of the ways in which the interpretation of the text makes possible deeper understanding of the wider issues, both historical and theological, with which the Bible is concerned. Select bibliographies in each volume point the way to further discussion of the many issues which remain open to fuller exploration.

P.R.A.
G.N.S.

NOTES

The Scripture quotations in this publication are from the New Revised Standard Version of the Bible copyrighted 1989 by the Division of Christian Education of the National Council of the Churches of Christ in the USA and used by permission.

Yahweh is an alternative translation of 'the Lord'.

BCE (before the common era) is used in preference to BC and CE (the common era) in preference to AD.

CONTENTS

KEY PASSAGES DISCUSSED

Genesis 2: 4—3: 24
Genesis 18: 22–33
Exodus 19: 1—Numbers 10: 28
Exodus 20: 23—23: 19
Exodus 20: 1–17
  (= Deuteronomy 5: 6–21)
Leviticus 17–26
Deuteronomy 12–26
2 Samuel 11–20; 1 Kings 1–2
1 Kings 4: 29–34
2 Kings 22–3

Job 28
Proverbs 1–9
Proverbs 8: 22–31
Proverbs 10: 1—22: 16;
  25: 1—29: 27
Proverbs 22: 17–24: 34
Proverbs 30: 1–9
Ecclesiastes 12: 9–14
Daniel 1–6
Ecclesiasticus 24: 1–29
Wisdom 2: 1–9

Sages, Scribes, and Counsellors

The Writings: the third section of the Hebrew Bible

In the Hebrew Bible the books over and above Pentateuch and Prophets are listed simply as Writings (*ketubim* in Hebrew). The resulting tripartite distinction is first clearly attested in the Prologue to Ben Sira (Ecclesiasticus), written about 130 BCE by the author's grandson, which refers to 'the law, the prophets, and the other books of our fathers'. Ben Sira's own account of the scribal profession, to which he himself belonged, lists law, the wisdom of the ancients, and prophecy as the principal objects of study (39: 1). This is roughly what we find in the Hebrew Bible, though the sequence corresponds rather to the order in which the books are arranged in the Greek Bible or Septuagint. At any rate, this suggests that the formation of an authoritative collection of writings, later to be known as a canon, was well on its way by the second century BCE. It also suggests that this third section, the Writings, was meant to provide a cross-section of the accumulated wisdom of the past as a guide for living in the present; or, as Josephus would put it nearly three centuries later, 'precepts for the conduct of human life' (*Against Apion*, 1: 40).

Unlike the first two sections of the collection, however, the Writings do not exhibit any obvious principle of unity. From the literary point of view, they include historiography (1 and 2 Chronicles, Ezra, Nehemiah), edifying fiction (Esther, Daniel 1–6, Ruth), lyrics (Song of Songs), hymns (Psalms, Lamentations), dialogue (Job), monologue (Ecclesiastes), proverbs and aphorisms with other didactic genres (Proverbs), and apocalyptic (Daniel 7–12). The list will be even longer if we include books which came to be part of the Greek Bible. The common practice of referring to this heterogeneous collection as 'wisdom writings' would seem, then, to call for an explanation. Very few of these compositions (a core group of Job, Proverbs, Ecclesiastes) can be called sapiential in the sense of imparting instruction or addressing themselves to broad issues of a philosophical or theological nature. At the purely literary level, therefore, the designation 'wisdom writings' is clearly inadequate. The situation may, however, look rather different if we take into account the existence of an authoritative sapiential tradition within which a wide variety of literary forms, not in themselves obviously sapiential, could be located. A good example would be the Song of Songs.

On the face of it, this composition would appear to be a series of erotic poems in the courtly style, though the precise determination of its genre has long been in dispute. Impressed by the dialogue between courtesan and shepherd, some commentators have taken it to be a drama, perhaps with undertones of cultic drama associated with a fertility myth and celebrating the marriage of a male and female deity. For our purpose it is not important to decide this issue. What is important is that it is attributed to Solomon even though the fiction of Solomonic authorship is maintained only sporadically throughout the work. The reason for the attribution is, quite simply, that, by the time of writing, the tradition about Solomon as the embodiment of royal wisdom and the supreme example of the sage was firmly established. The point is made often in the biblical historian's account of Solomon's reign, written many centuries later. An important aspect of royal wisdom, illustrated by the well-known story of the two women claiming the same child (1 Kgs. 3: 16–28), had to do with the administration of justice, the most important function of monarchy. Another facet is shown in the visit of the Queen of Sheba to Solomon's court, during which he successfully answered the riddles she put to him (1 Kgs. 10: 1–10), thus demonstrating that his wisdom was equal to that of the Arabs, proverbial for sagacity. (The story may, in fact, be based on a trade mission from the southern Arabian peninsula.) The historian sums it up as follows:

God gave Solomon very great wisdom, discernment, and breadth of understanding, as vast as the sand on the seashore, so that Solomon's wisdom surpassed the wisdom of all the people of the east . . . and his fame spread throughout all the surrounding nations . . . He composed three thousand proverbs, and his songs numbered a thousand and five. He would speak of trees, from the cedar that is in the Lebanon to the hyssop that grows in the wall; he would speak of animals, and birds, and reptiles, and fish. People came from all the nations to hear the wisdom of Solomon; they came from all the kings of the earth who had heard of his wisdom.   (1 Kgs. 4: 29–34)

The title, 'the Song of Songs which is Solomon's' implies, therefore, the writer's intent to present it as the most excellent of the thousand and five composed by Solomon. And since Solomon's wisdom, which included literary ability, came to him as a divine gift bestowed in a vision (related in 1 Kgs. 3: 4–14), there is the further implication of divine inspiration. To attribute a book to Solomon, then, was a way of bringing it within the sapiential tradition and bestowing on it a special authority. Thus, the two longer collections of aphorisms in the Book of Proverbs are presented as a selection of the three thousand which Solomon uttered (Prov. 10: 1; 25: 1), and the book itself was published under his name (Prov. 1: 1). Despite some disconcerting views which it expresses, Ecclesiastes (Qoheleth) found its way into the collection under the same imprimatur. The tradition was carried on in the Wisdom of Solomon, the Odes of Solomon, and, eventually, in the esoteric writings of Jewish (and other) cabbalists and mystics into the Middle Ages and beyond.

We therefore conclude that the Song of Songs, though not a didactic composition in any obvious sense, was seen to contain a message which the sages wished to recommend with all the authority of an age-old tradition. Without going into the interpretation of the book, in dispute since late antiquity, we simply note how it gives pride of place to the mystery and power of love between woman and man; this much at least is clear. The point is made in the one generalizing statement in the book, towards the end, clearly an editorial addition:

> Many waters cannot quench love,
>   neither can floods drown it.
> If one offered for love
>   all the wealth of his house,
>   it would be utterly scorned.   (8: 7)

In spite of the many Old Testament proverbs which exhibit an ungenerous and petulant attitude to women, the frank acceptance of erotic love is by no means foreign to the tradition in which the writer or editor stood. There is the numerical proverb (Prov. 30: 18–19), to be discussed in the next chapter, about the way of a man with a maid, and there is the question addressed to the young man tempted to adultery:

> Can fire be carried in the bosom
> without burning one's clothes?   (Prov. 6: 27)

Indeed, at one point in Proverbs we find the same kind of imagery, euphemisms, and 'conceits' as in the Song of Songs:

> Drink water from your own cistern,
> flowing water from your own well.
> Should your springs be scattered abroad,
> streams of water in the streets? . . .
> Let your fountain be blessed,
> and rejoice in the wife of your youth,
> a lovely deer, a graceful doe.
> May her breasts satisfy you at all times;
> may you be intoxicated always by her love.
> (Prov. 5: 15–19)

We do not have to choose between this way of interpreting the Song of Songs and that other way, found so often in Jewish and Christian mystical writings, which refers the sexual imagery to the bond between God and Israel as his spouse. Given the development of the theme of a divine marriage covenant in the eighth-century prophet Hosea, and the powerful influence which it continued to exert, the reference was surely inevitable. In this respect it may be significant that Hosea is the only prophetic book which ends with a colophon couched in the language of the sages:

> Those who are wise understand these things;
> Those who are discerning know them.   (14: 9)

The development of this sapiential or intellectual–religious tradition, in its Israelite–Judean stage up to the Babylonian exile in the sixth century BCE, and in its early Jewish stage from then onwards, follows along the same lines as the formation of the biblical canon.

According to the traditional account, the canon of the Hebrew Scriptures was fixed by Ezra and the men of the Great Assembly, a legislative body which included the last of the prophets, i.e., Haggai, Zechariah, Malachi, and other worthies, one hundred and twenty in all. Any doubts remaining thereafter about individual books, including the Song of Songs, were laid to rest at a synod held at Jamnia (Yavneh), the intellectual centre of Judaism after the disastrous war with Rome, towards the end of the first century CE. This traditional account of the formation of the canon has rightly been abandoned by critical scholarship, but it may serve to indicate the important role played in this process by the scribes, represented by Ezra, and their successors, the leaders of the early rabbinic academies. At a later point we shall see how the influence and prestige of the scribal schools steadily increased, especially after they took over the drafting and interpreting of the laws. There are also indications, to be noted in due course, that the sages took over the prophetic claim to mediate revelation, leading to the rabbinic statement that prophecy has been taken from the prophets and given to the sages. It was by virtue of such a claim that the biblical canon came to be expanded to cover a miscellaneous body of writings over and above the Law and the Prophets.

The many faces of wisdom

Before going much further we need to ask: What is this elusive quality called 'wisdom'? What, following these biblical texts, does it mean to be wise? If we survey the relevant vocabulary in the Hebrew Bible, we will see that very often wisdom (*ḥokmah* in Hebrew) signifies the possession of a particular skill, e.g. that of the goldsmith (Jer. 10: 9), stonemason (1 Chr. 22: 15), or shipbuilder (Ezek. 27: 8–9). Bezalel and his colleagues who were commissioned to make the tent and the ark were 'wise' in the sense that they were endowed with the necessary technical and artistic skills (Exod. 31: 1–11; 35: 30—36: 1). A special case would be that of the magician's art (e.g. Isa. 3: 3) corresponding to the kind of competence expected of sages in ancient Egypt, at least as the Israelites viewed them (Gen. 41: 8; Exod. 7: 11). As for those 'wise women' mentioned here and there in the record (2 Sam. 14: 2; 20: 16), the emphasis seems to be more on persuasive speech than the magical arts. One might say that they were closer to running a counselling agency than practising witch-craft. One of them was hired by the army commander to persuade David to permit Absalom's return (2 Sam. 14: 1–20), and the other talked a different commander into raising the siege of a city (2 Sam. 20: 14–22). Following well-established precedent, however, wisdom *par excellence* belonged to the ruler. The first of the two wise women just mentioned seems to have been well acquainted with this convention in ascribing to David 'wisdom like the angel of God to know all things that are on the earth' (2 Sam. 14: 20). And in the person of his son Solomon, as we have seen, royal wisdom reached its fullest expression.

One of the great crises in the early history of Israel was the estab-lishment of a monarchy and the entire apparatus of state control that went with it, beginning with David and Solomon but not fully in place until at least a century later. Centralized administration required for its operation a corps of personnel—scribes, secretaries, recorders, counsellors—who had to be educated and socialized into the internationally accepted ethos and etiquette of public life. Much of the instructional and aphoristic material in Proverbs was written with this educational purpose in view. It was no doubt inevitable that tension and conflict should arise between this new 'wisdom' of inter-national stamp on the one hand and the traditional religious ideas and practices (e.g. appeal to an oracle or a seer for guidance) of a tribal and regional culture on the other. The tension is fully in evi-dence in the court history covering the last years of David's reign (2 Sam. 11–20; 1 Kgs. 1–2), one of the great masterpieces of Hebrew prose, and the symbolic narrative about the man, the woman, and the snake in the Garden of Eden (Gen. 2: 4—3: 24). A brief look at these two compositions is in order.

The court history tells how, against all the odds, Solomon suc-ceeded to David's throne. The first episode narrates David's adul-tery with Bathsheba, the murder in cold blood of the unsuspecting husband, probably with the connivance of Bathsheba, the interven-tion of the prophet Nathan, and the birth and death of a first child followed by the conception and birth of Solomon (2 Sam. 11–12). The final episode, in which the last rival is eliminated and which features the same cast of characters (David, Bathsheba, Nathan, Solomon), neatly rounds off the story (1 Kgs. 1–2). The second episode deals with Amnon, the crown prince and first in line to the throne (2 Sam. 13). Wishing to possess himself of his beautiful half-sister Tamar, he sought advice of David's nephew Jonadab described as 'a very wise man' (13: 3). Jonadab's wisdom turned out to be the kind of guile which enabled him to propose a plan whereby Amnon could have his will of Tamar. The plan worked, but it led to the death of Amnon, assassinated by Absalom as he lay in a drunken stupor. In due course Absalom, exiled from the court as a result of avenging his sister's honour, was brought back by the wiles of a 'wise woman' hired by the army commander Joab (2 Sam. 14). This too had fateful consequences, leading to Absalom's rebellion and, eventually, his death in battle. A dominant theme, therefore, is the intervention of a wise or ostensibly wise agent which ends not in enlightenment but in disaster and death.

The paradox of this kind of lethal wisdom is exemplified most vividly in the person of Ahithophel, David's counsellor, who joined Absalom's conspiracy and rebellion. His prestige was such that 'the counsel that Ahithophel gave was as if one consulted the oracle of God' (16: 23). David prayed to Yahweh to turn that counsel into foolishness (15: 31), and the subsequent course of the narrative shows how the prayer was answered. Ahithophel's advice, to attack David at once before he had time to consolidate his position, was sound, but it was countered by that of Hushai, another sage left behind by David to deceive the unsuspecting Absalom. At this point the writer makes one of his infrequent intrusions into the story with the comment that

Yahweh had ordained to defeat the good counsel of Ahithophel, so that Yahweh might bring ruin on Absalom. (17: 14)

The episode then comes to an end with Ahithophel's suicide (17: 23).

The ambiguities of wisdom are illustrated in a remarkably similar way in the Garden of Eden narrative, part of the so-called Primeval History (Gen. 1–11). While the mythic topoi employed by the writer can be shown to derive from ancient Mesopotamia, a Canaanite version existed and was used by Ezekiel in his lamentation over the king of Tyre (Ezek. 28: 12–19). It would, however, be misleading to describe the story in Genesis simply as a myth. It is, rather, an excellent example of the ability of the sages to make learned use of mythological tradition for their own ends or, as Plato put it, to philosophize by means of myth. In other respects, too, the sapiential character of the narrative is apparent; suffice it to note the interest in ancient geography (the four rivers, 2: 10–14) and the Man's naming of the animals (2: 19–20), an anticipation or reflection of Solomon's onomastic wisdom, that is, his skill in naming, and therefore ordering, things (1 Kgs. 4: 33). As in Ezekiel's poem, the Man who is to lose his innocence for ever starts out 'full of wisdom, perfect in beauty'.

With the entry of the serpent into the story, we have another example of a wise agent following whose advice leads to ruinous consequences. The function of the serpent is expressed in a punning use of the Hebrew words *'arom/ 'arum* (naked/cunning):

The man and his wife were both *'arumim* (naked), and were not ashamed; now the serpent was more *'arum* (naked/crafty) than any other wild creature that Yahweh God had made.   (2: 25—3: 1)

In a sense, of course, snakes are naked or hairless in contrast to most other animals. They are also represented in ancient Near Eastern myth and iconography as both symbolizing the phallus and bringing secret knowledge and wisdom, including magical knowledge and knowledge of healing, out of the earth where they live. In the story, the snake's strategy is to get the woman, and through her the man, to eat of the tree of knowledge of good and evil. Commentators have ranged far and wide in an attempt to determine the meaning of this phrase and, therefore, the symbolic function of the tree. For our present purpose the story tells us all we need to know, namely, that the tree was capable of conferring wisdom (3: 6). The implication is that the couple did in fact obtain wisdom, but a wisdom which brought on them the judgement of mortality.

Both the court history in Samuel and the story in Genesis acknowledge the reality and the power of a wisdom which relies exclusively on human resources and autonomous reason. It is a wisdom that really works, but these narratives also reflect the anxious knowledge that to follow it is to risk alienation from the God who called Israel into existence and gave her her destiny. The ensuing tension—apparent, for example, in the prophetic polemic against royal counsellors (Isa. 5: 18–23; 29: 14; 30: 1–2)—remained a prominent feature of public life during the monarchy.

The professional sage

The professional dispenser of wisdom in the ancient Near East belonged to a small and privileged élite with a high sense of its own calling. A text from ancient Egypt says of scribes that 'their mortuary service is gone; their tombstones are covered with dirt; and their graves are forgotten. But their names are still pronounced because of their books which they made, since they were good, and the memory of him who made them lasts to the limits of eternity.' Another Egyptian classic, from the late third or early second millennium, contrasts a range of other occupations—barber, construction worker, gardener—unfavourably with the scribe and concludes, 'behold, there is no profession free of a boss—except for the scribe: he is the boss'. In the same vein Ben Sira—a rather snobbish individual, one suspects—reserves the pursuit of wisdom to the leisured class to which he himself belonged:

> The wisdom of the scribe depends on the opportunity of leisure;
>   only the one who has little business can become wise.
> How can one become wise who handles the plough,
>   and who glories in the shaft of a goad,
> who drives oxen and is occupied with their work,
>   and whose talk is about bulls?   (Ecclus. 38: 24–5)

Compared with prophets and priests, we know very little about a class of sages during the time of the monarchy; there is in fact some doubt as to whether such a class existed. While the term *hakam* (wise, sage) is used of many individuals, it is rarely possible to read into it a reference to a distinct category, class, or profession. There are, by contrast, many allusions to foreign sages. Those of Egypt are skilled in dream interpretation (Gen. 41: 8) and the magical arts (Exod. 7: 11) and serve as counsellors to pharaohs (Isa. 19: 11–12). Much the same can be said of Babylonian sages (Jer. 50: 35; 51: 57; Dan. 2: 12, etc.) and those of other lands noted for their wisdom, such as Phoenicia and Edom. Public officials and royal counsellors in Israel thought of themselves as wise, and may have been known collectively as *ḥakamim*, though the claim did not go uncontested (e.g. Isa. 5: 18–23; 29: 14). Perhaps the nearest we come to a specific class of *ḥakamim* is in the words attributed to those who conspired against Jeremiah: 'Come, let us make plots against Jeremiah—for instruction shall not perish from the priest, nor counsel from the wise, nor the word from the prophet' (18: 18; cf. Ezek. 7: 26 which has 'elders' for 'wise'). Thus, counsel, professional advice, was the province of the sage as instruction in the laws was that of the priest. The general impression, then, is that with the passage to monarchy there came into existence a class of royal counsellors or cabinet ministers whose responsibility was to give wise counsel and who were referred to generically as 'wise' (*ḥakamim*). Note, finally, the practice of putting together 'sayings of the sages' attested in Proverbs (22: 17, cf. 25: 1) and Qoheleth (12: 11), a practice which continued down into the Roman period and beyond.

One quite distinctive profession included under the generic rubric of 'sage' was that of the scribe (*soper*). As the name suggests, the basic responsibility of this official was to write; a not unimportant task at a time when writing was a specialist occupation. From the earliest period of the monarchy nothing much is known about them except their names (2 Sam. 8: 16–17; 20: 25; 1 Kgs. 4: 3; 2 Kgs. 12: 10). It appears, however, that they played an important role in matters of state, serving on royal commissions, overseeing the running of the temple, taking part in diplomatic missions and negotiations with foreign powers, drafting royal edicts, and supervising tax returns. The best-known examples are Shebna during the reign of Hezekiah (2 Kgs. 18–19; Isa. 22: 15–25) and Shaphan who had an equally distinguished career in the service of Josiah (2 Kgs. 22). The royal scribe occupied a post of broader and more official responsibility than that of counsellors such as Ahithophel and Hushai, though both scribe and counsellor came within the vaguer category of 'the wise'. The milieu of this kind of wisdom, then, was the royal court and its dependents.

The historian of the monarchy records that, during the reign of Josiah (640–609 BCE), the high priest discovered a law book in the course of carrying out repairs to the temple fabric and that, after authentication by a female prophet, this law was officially promulgated in Jerusalem (2 Kgs. 22: 8—23: 3). The identity and origin of the law in question, and especially the issue of its relationship with Deuteronomy, will be dealt with in Chapter 4. What needs to be said now is that laws require interpretation and therefore necessarily call into existence a class of legal specialists. It is hardly coincidental that we hear of such specialists for the first time from Jeremiah whose early activity coincided with the promulgation of the Josian–Deuteronomic law. The reference is neither friendly nor complimentary:

> The priests did not say, 'Where is Yahweh?'
> Those who handle the law did not know me;
> the rulers transgressed against me . . . (Jer. 2: 8)

This category—handlers of or specialists in the law—is therefore distinct from the priests who from the earliest times were the custodians of the legal tradition. It may, in fact, have come into existence as a specialization of the priestly function. Elsewhere Jeremiah castigates those who claim to be wise on the grounds of possessing a *written* law and suggests that its meaning had been perverted by this kind of scribal activity:

> How can you say, 'We are wise,
> and the law of Yahweh is with us'?
> when, in fact, the false pen of the scribes
> has made it into a lie?
> The wise shall be put to shame,
> they shall be dismayed and taken;
> since they have rejected the word of Yahweh,
> what wisdom is in them? (8: 8–9)

The implication seems to be that a class of professional legal experts—no doubt identical with the 'handlers of the law' mentioned earlier—was offering authoritative interpretations of the laws and that this activity was seen by Jeremiah to pose a threat to his authority as prophet. What was at stake, therefore, was control of the 'redemptive media' in the society and therefore of the conscience of the community. These scribes were quite distinct from the royal officials whom we have just discussed. They may be connected with the central judiciary set up by the Deuteronomic law (Deut. 17: 8–13), but the new and disturbing element for Jeremiah was the claim that the will of Yahweh could be circumscribed by a written law and its authoritative interpretations to the exclusion of the prophetic word. No prophet could let that go unchallenged.

This saying of Jeremiah gives us our first reference to law scribes as a distinct category. After the restoration of the Judaean community in the Persian period (sixth to fourth century BCE) they were to assume increasing importance. According to the Chronicler, our principal source for the period, they belonged for the most part to the clerical ranks. At the great assembly convened by Ezra for the reading of the law book, the necessary legal commentary and interpretation were supplied by Levites, a clerical order subordinate to the sacrificing priesthood (Neh. 8: 7–8). In his retelling of the history of the monarchy the author of 1–2 Chronicles also represents levitical scribes as active during the reign of David (1 Chr. 24: 6) and Josiah (2 Chr. 34: 13), and at a later point has Levites touring the country giving instruction in the law (2 Chr. 17: 7–9). Ezra himself is described as both priest and scribe and his principal concern is the study of the law (Ezra 7: 10 etc.). Later still, the scribe Ben Sira is first and foremost a legal scholar (Ecclus. 32: 14–15; 39: 1) and teaches his discipline in a school (51: 23). Other teachers and sages were active during this long period, including Qoheleth and those whose sayings were brought together by the editor of Proverbs (1: 6; 22: 17; 24: 33; 30: 1; 31: 1). Increasingly, however, the interpretation of and instruction in the law took centre stage and became the vital link with Judaism of the post-biblical period.

Education in Israel

It will be apparent from the previous section that the sages of Israel were primarily teachers. The literature which they produced itself attests to this. Proverbs 13: 14, for example, describes the teaching of the wise as a fountain of life, and the epilogue to Ecclesiastes (Qoheleth), from a later hand, identifies the author explicitly as a teacher (12: 9). The prologue to Proverbs states quite clearly that the purpose of the collection is educational:

> For learning about wisdom and instruction,
>   for understanding words of insight,
> for gaining instruction in wise dealing,
>   righteousness, justice and equity;
> to teach shrewdness to the simple,
>   knowledge and prudence to the young . . .
>
> (1: 2–4)

Since, therefore, the 'wisdom' of which the texts speak had to be taught, it may be useful to summarize what little is known of education in Israel before going on to examine the literature in detail.

To begin on a rather discouraging note, we have practically no information on the education of the young in the period preceding the establishment of the state. In a participatory society based on subsistence agriculture and the raising of livestock, and in which the basic structures were those of kinship, the kind of educational apparatus with which we are familiar today was neither possible nor necessary. All that was needed to equip the young with the skills required to survive and function in that kind of society was provided by the extended family, the household and the clan. In that kind of social system the mother played the essential educative role of socializing the child and inculcating the traditional ethos in the form of story, parable, aphorism, and precept. In the public sphere the elders played the dominant role, above all in judicial matters. Even if formulated at a later time, allusions to things that are 'not done in Israel' (e.g. 2 Sam. 13: 12), and injunctions to pass on and explain religious traditions to children (e.g. Exod. 12: 26–7), reflect the situation which obtained before the emergence of the state. And to anticipate a point that will be taken up in a later chapter, the traditional ethos of the kinship group stands at the origins of both the sapiential–didactic and the legal tradition in Israel.

We should perhaps allow for the possibility that proximity to one or other of the Late Bronze Age Canaanite cities provided an opportunity for a more formal kind of education, limited, of course, to the social and economic élite. A tablet discovered at Shechem in the Central Highlands, dating from the beginning of the fourteenth century, records the complaint of a teacher (who refers to himself as 'father') addressed to a parent delinquent in the payment of fees. An agricultural calendar inscribed on a small limestone tablet, discovered at Gezer in 1908 and generally dated to the early monarchy, has been widely interpreted as a schoolboy's exercise, though this is no more than a guess. All we can say is that there is no hard evidence for educational institutions at that time, or much later, as opposed to one-to-one teaching and learning. The discovery of a few lines or a sequence of letters of the alphabet (abecedaries) scratched on stone or pottery (e.g. at Gezer, Lachish, Arad, Khirbet el-Qom) does not require us to postulate schools. Unlike Mesopotamian cuneiform or Egyptian hieroglyphic, the Hebrew alphabetic script consisting of twenty-two letters could easily be taught by a parent or scribe without the need for extended, formal instruction.

Needless to say, the most important and basic skill was writing. Essential for the conduct of diplomacy, it was also increasingly required for the administration of law and estate management. In the Sumerian city-states writing was taught in scribal schools as early as the third millennium BCE. The literary remains recovered from such centres (Uruk, Shuruppak, etc.), including proverbs, fables, precepts, and student exercises, necessarily presuppose such institutions. The same situation obtained in Egypt where the scribal profession was held in the highest honour. The thousands of tablets recovered from ancient Ugarit (Ras Shamra) on the Syrian coast, closer to ancient Israel both geographically and culturally, provide indications pointing in the same direction. Unfortunately, we do not have comparable evidence from Late Bronze Age Canaan. Unlike the great riverine and maritime centres, early Israel was a derivative, non-urban society, and therefore one in which we would not expect, and do not find, a comparable level of literacy and literary culture. When it was necessary for the ordinary individual to draft a contract, or lodge a complaint in writing, or something of the sort, he or she would have to pay a scribe the going rate to have it done. We have one example of such a document written on behalf of a day-labourer to the military governor at Yavneh-Yam (Meṣad Hashavyahu) near Tel Aviv during the reign of Josiah (640–609 BCE). It begins, 'let my lord the governor hear the word of his servant', and goes on to request an official intervention to restore a confiscated garment.

The change to monarchy led, as we have seen, to the demand for trained personnel to serve the state in a variety of capacities. Of the state officials mentioned in the history one of the most important was the scribe (*soper*) noted earlier in this chapter. The scribe was, of course, trained to write, and there are allusions to such tools of the trade as the scribe's pen (Jer. 8: 8), penknife for sharpening quills (36: 23) and writing case (Ezek. 9: 2–3). We have already noted, however, that his (less commonly her) competence went far beyond writing, including skill in public speaking, negotiation with foreign powers, and financial administration. From the historian's account of the parleying under the gates of Jerusalem while the Assyrians were besieging the city in 701 BCE (2 Kgs. 18: 26), during the reign of Hezekiah, it also appears that scribes could be expected to know the diplomatic language of the period, in this case Aramaic. There are indications that the royal scribe exercised some jurisdiction over the state cult (2 Kgs. 12: 10; 22: 3–10), the temple had its own scribes (Jer. 36: 10–12, 20–1; 37: 15) and so did the army (2 Kgs. 25: 19). Personal scribes or secretaries were probably quite rare, but a scribe named Baruch was employed by Jeremiah, wrote his sayings from dictation, and read them from a scroll in the temple (Jer. 36). All of this is unintelligible without some kind of school for scribes in Jerusalem, perhaps established on the model of the Egyptian temple-college known as the 'house of life', in which the sons of the élite were prepared to play a role in public life.

Since, therefore, the scribal schools existed to prepare the sons of the well-to-do for public service or a life at court, the emphasis would have been on correct comportment, etiquette, and public speaking. The literary models used for training, beginning with literary competence, were probably translated from Egyptian or Akkadian (the Semitic language spoken in the Euphrates–Tigris basin), or at least based on school texts written in those languages. For the content of that instruction we have to rely almost exclusively on the biblical texts, especially the Book of Proverbs. There is practically nothing in the archaeological record, for the simple and sad reason that papyrus, the preferred writing surface for texts of any length, has a hard time surviving the Palestinian winter. With the exception of a clump of papyrus fibres attached to the seal of a certain Gedaliah found at Lachish, only one papyrus, discovered some years ago in the Wadi Muraba ʿat, has in fact survived from the time of the monarchy.

To judge by the didactic material which has come down to us in Judean (Proverbs), Egyptian, and Mesopotamian texts, the instruction imparted to these aspiring civil servants would have emphasized such things as self-control, learning from experience, drawing lessons from the observation of nature, avoiding compromising situations, and the like. There was nothing particularly religious about it, and so it is not surprising that the political pragmatism and rationality of officials trained in this way inevitably came into conflict with the claims and demands of those prophets who, like Isaiah and Jeremiah, were deeply involved in the political affairs of the nation. We rarely encounter this kind of situation today, but the struggle during the Iranian revolution between the modernizing party and the Imams with their radical commitment to Islam may give us some idea of what was involved.

With the loss of national independence after the Babylonian conquest and fall of Jerusalem (587 or 586 BCE), the vacuum created by the disappearance of the monarchy was filled to a great extent by the priesthood. In the texts which have survived from the period of the restoration, after the Persian conquest permitted and encouraged a return to the province of Judah, the emphasis is on the study and observance of the laws. According to 1 and 2 Chronicles, together with Ezra–Nehemiah; our principal source for the two centuries of Persian imperial control, the scribe is now a teacher and a preacher, and what he teaches and preaches is law, Torah. Whatever the political status of Ezra as emissary of the Persian government, it is his role as student, exponent, and teacher of the law which is emphasized in the account of his mission to Judah, probably in 458 BCE (Ezra 7). The purpose of the mission was to see that the 'law of the God of heaven' was known and observed in the province of Judah, indeed in the entire satrapy 'Beyond the River' (Ezra 7: 25), and this goal involved an educational mission. Whatever its historical character, the great assembly at which the law book was read by Ezra and explained by Levites, as recorded in Nehemiah 8, probably reflects the actual practice of the Chronicler's own day; and the same could be said of his description of levitical scribes going from town to town giving instruction in the law (2 Chr. 17: 7–9).

By the time of Ben Sira in the second century BCE the 'house of study' was a well-established institution in the cities and possibly also in the villages. Little as we know of the origins and early development of the synagogue, the indications are that from the earliest times it served as an educational centre as well as a place of prayer and worship. 'Profane' learning was certainly available in the Hellenistic cities in Palestine and beyond for those Jews who had the means and the disposition to pursue it, and many Jewish authors both before and after the time of Ben Sira elected to write in Greek. But the basic education, at least for traditional Jews, was in Torah. Thus Josephus, a well-educated man if no great thinker, informs us in his autobiography that 'while still a mere boy, about fourteen years old, I won universal applause for my love of letters; insomuch that the chief priests and the leading men of the city used constantly to come to me for precise information on some particular in our ordinances'. Another Pharisee, Paul, was also well versed in Torah and the various exegetical procedures then in use for the interpretation of Scripture. And while Josephus and Paul were hardly typical Pharisees, we are reminded that it was the Pharisees who, more than others, promoted Torah-learning among the people.

Many of the points made in this brief summary will be further developed and illustrated in subsequent chapters. Our main purpose will be to trace the two great streams of wisdom and law from their sources to the point where they flow together and eventually find their outlet in the rabbinic writings and early Christian theology. The first and essential stage is, of course, the understanding of the relevant biblical texts themselves, and to these we now turn.

Education for Life

Proverbs: the book

Proverbs is a manual of didactic material, a source book of instruction containing several distinct compilations brought together and edited from a specific religious viewpoint some time during the period of the Second Temple. Despite the fact that some parts of the collection are attributed to specific individuals—e.g. Hezekiah's men (25: 1), Agur (30: 1), Lemuel (31: 1)—the work as a whole comes to us under the name of Solomon (1: 1). No one doubts, however, that this is a pseudonym, the result of a long-standing tradition of regarding Solomon as fountainhead of wisdom in all of its aspects including literary skill (1 Kgs. 4: 32). The attribution may, at any rate, serve to remind us that Proverbs may well contain genuinely ancient material, providing us with a cross-section of Israelite wisdom in its many historical phases over a period of several centuries.

The individual compositions or compilations in the book are fairly easy to disengage since almost all of them have titles. They may be set out as follows:

1. An instruction on wisdom and folly (1: 8—9: 18).
2. A 'Solomonic' collection of proverbs (10: 1—22: 16).
3. A collection entitled 'Sayings of the Wise' (22: 17—24: 22).
4. A supplementary collection with the same title (24: 23–34).
5. A second 'Solomonic' collection edited by Hezekiah's scribes (25: 1—29: 27).
6. Sayings of Agur (30: 1–9).
7. A collection of mostly numerical sayings (30: 10–33).
8. Sayings of Lemuel (31: 1–9).

9. Acrostic (alphabetic) poem on the 'woman of substance' (31: 10–31).

The anthology is introduced as 'Proverbs of Solomon', which is understandable in view of the fact that the two collections of 'Solomonic' proverbs (2 and 5) make up by far the largest part of the material in the book. It was noted in the previous chapter that the prologue (1: 2–7) presents the book as a manual for the education of the young. It concludes on an explicitly religious note with the reminder that

> The fear of Yahweh is the beginning of knowledge;
> fools despise wisdom and instruction.   (1: 7)

If this comes from a later hand, as several commentators suggest, it would not be the only instance where the teaching of the sages has been brought into line with Yahwistic piety (cf. Prov. 14: 27; Eccles. 12: 13; Job 28: 28). Alternating with the two major collections of proverbs are two instructions (1, 3–4), the latter (22: 17—24: 34) being an Israelite adaptation of the Egyptian Wisdom of Amen-em-opet, as will be seen in greater detail at a later point. The final section, praising the good wife, is meant to correspond to the figure of the Woman called Wisdom presented in the first section. It was quite common in antiquity to round off a work in a way calculated to recall its opening.

That the book represents the effort of a Second Temple editor to bring together a cross-section of scribal wisdom covering a long period of time is apparent not only in the variety of the material included but also in the titles. Some of the parts are anonymous ('Sayings of the Wise'), some pseudonymous ('Proverbs of Solomon'), and others attributed to named individuals (Agur, Lemuel). Anonymity is normal in the ancient world. Pseudonymity arises in response to the need to legitimate and confer authority on a composition by linking it with a normative history and a great figure in the tradition. So, for example, Deuteronomy is attributed to Moses and Psalms to David. The practice of putting one's name to a book is attested only towards the end of the biblical period, the earliest extant example being Jesus ben Sira (Ecclus. 50: 27). While the sayings of Agur and Lemuel are the exception in Proverbs in this respect, by the time of the Mishnah (*c*.200 CE) it was common practice for sayings to be attributed to individual sages some of whom lived within the biblical period.

The proverb

It will be clear from both the title and content of the book that the proverb was the most characteristic form in which the sages and teachers of Israel gave instruction and expressed their understanding of human existence. While etymology is at best an imperfect guide to meaning, it may be worth noting that the Hebrew word *mashal* is associated by some with a word-group connoting 'rule' or 'power' and by others with the idea of 'comparison' or 'model'. Those who take the first option wish to emphasize the originally magical, incantatory, and performative function of expressive language, while the alternative of 'model' or 'paradigm' will lead to stressing the representational and metaphoric function. If, however, we attend to actual usage, we see that *mashal* can stand for a wide variety of literary forms in Proverbs and elsewhere in the Hebrew Bible. It can be used for prophetic oracles, such as the enigmatic utterances of Balaam the seer (Num. 23: 7), and can also connote a taunt (Jer. 24: 9) or an allegory (Ezek. 17: 2). Note, too, that Job dismisses the well-worn, traditional arguments of his colleagues as 'proverbs of ashes' (Job 13: 12). In its characteristic form, however, it denotes *a brief, pointed saying, concrete in its imagery and general in its applicability, related in some way to human character and conduct*. This is the type that we find in the two long collections attributed to Solomon in the book.

A comparativist approach to the proverb will help us see more clearly some of the ways in which it functions in different social situations. In general, a particular society's stock of proverbs represents a deposit of the accumulated wisdom of the past, a distillation of collective experience based on the observation of order, regularity, and causality in nature and in human affairs. Together with traditional narrative or folktale, the corpus of proverbs in a traditional society serves to transmit its inherited values, thus helping to form the basis for an agreed pattern of behaviour against which the conduct of the individual can be measured and with reference to which social deviance can be discouraged. In many societies (e.g. tribal societies in Nigeria) proverbs also play an important role in the administration of justice. Since both proverbial lore and case or common law are based on precedent and draw their authority from the transmitted wisdom of the past, it is hardly surprising that in Israel the sapiential and legal traditions are so closely connected.

We have seen that the proverb, by definition, must be brief and pointed. Very often its longevity is a function of its internal rhyme ('a stitch in time saves nine'; 'birds of a feather flock together') or alliteration ('look before you leap') or some other striking quality. Proverbs will generally, perhaps universally, be anonymous; hence the much-quoted 'early to bed, early to rise, makes a man healthy, wealthy and wise', attributed to Benjamin Franklin, is not a genuine proverb, besides being demonstrably false. Precisely because they are traditional and long-lived, proverbs will also often reflect the social situation of a past age. We still admonish people not to count their chickens before they are hatched, though few of us raise chickens. Relatively few current proverbial sayings, therefore, reflect an urban, post-industrial environment.

Quite a few proverbial expressions, of the short, pithy kind, can be found scattered throughout the Hebrew Bible. Examples such as the following could be found in practically any society: 'As the man is, so is his strength' (Judg. 8: 21), 'Out of the wicked comes forth wickedness' (1 Sam. 24: 13), 'Let not him who girds on his armour boast as he who puts it off' (1 Kgs. 20: 11), 'Like mother, like daughter' (Ezek. 16: 44). Others have a more specific historical point of reference: 'Like Nimrod, a mighty hunter before Yahweh' (Gen. 10: 9), 'Is Saul also among the prophets?' (1 Sam. 10: 11; 19: 24), 'Let them but ask counsel at Abel' (2 Sam. 20: 18). These last we recognize as proverbial sayings only because the context describes them as such, though it is doubtful whether they should be classified as proverbs at all. We are, of course, familiar with proverbs containing a local reference (e.g. 'carrying coals to Newcastle'), but these are making a point of general applicability, and therefore are often adapted to different situations (e.g. 'bringing owls to Athens'). This does not seem to be the case with the kind of proverb just quoted from biblical narrative.

In other instances, especially in prophetic books, it can be equally difficult to decide whether we are dealing with a genuine proverb or a rhetorical device. Examples would be Isaiah's 'Let us eat and drink, for tomorrow we die' (22: 13) or Jeremiah's question, 'What has straw in common with wheat?' (23: 28). A very rare case of a bicolon or two-member proverb comes from the time very shortly before or after the fall of Jerusalem: 'The parents have eaten sour grapes, and the children's teeth are set on edge' (Jer. 31: 29; Ezek. 18: 2). Originally embodying the not uncommon complaint that the present generation is suffering for the mistakes of its predecessors, this proverbial saying came to voice the accusation that God was using the Babylonians to punish his people for the sins of their ancestors.

It is this kind of elaborated, literary kind of proverb that we find in the two major collections in the Book of Proverbs. With few exceptions, these proverbs conform to a fixed type: a compact, two-member unit in verse, in the parallel arrangement typical of Hebrew poetry. The stylization and elaboration evident in this form do not suggest a popular folk origin, though it is sometimes possible to detect popular usage behind the literary elaboration. But in general they are not popular but scholastic, and their intent is explicitly didactic. The bicolon (two-member) structure also has the advantage of allowing the play of different kinds of relationship between the two cola without sacrificing that unity of form and content which is characteristic of the proverb. In some it is a case of a simple and explicit comparison:

> Like vinegar to the teeth, and smoke to the eyes,
>   so are the lazy to their employers.   (10: 26)

or

> Like the cold of snow in the time of harvest
>   are faithful messengers to those who send them.   (25: 13)

In others the comparison is implicit, and the proverb, therefore, a kind of extended metaphor:

> Iron sharpens iron,
>   and one person sharpens the wits of another.   (27: 17)

A quite common form of juxtaposition occurs when we pass from the observation of regularity in nature in the first colon to the moral order in the second:

> The north wind brings rain,
>> and a backbiting tongue, angry looks.   (25: 23)

or

> For lack of wood the fire goes out,
>> and where there is no whisperer, quarreling ceases.
>>> (26: 20)

This type illustrates one of the basic goals of the sages in Israel and elsewhere in the ancient Near East: to bring human conduct into line with a cosmic law of regularity and order observable in the sequence of seasons, the movements of the heavenly bodies and the like. To be wise is, in a word, to live in conformity with the law of nature. It also shows how a moral consensus is built up in a traditional society such as early Israel on conclusions drawn from repeated observation, e.g., of the kinds of situations calculated to generate anger, resentment, and dissension.

As in Hebrew poetry in general, the parallelism characteristic of these proverbs can be of different kinds. An example of synonymous parallelism would be:

> Even fools who keep silent are considered wise;
>> when they close their lips, they are deemed intelligent.
>>> (17: 28)

—rather like the old Roman maxim, 'If you had kept quiet you would have passed for a philosopher'. Or, again:

> Even in laughter the heart is sad,
>> and the end of joy is grief.   (14: 13)

—one of the few instances in Proverbs which touch on the deeper, more baffling and paradoxical aspects of human existence. More common than these, however, is the kind which makes its point by contrast or antithesis:

> A wise child makes a glad father,
>> but a foolish child is a mother's grief.   (10: 1)

or

> Hatred stirs up strife,
>> but love covers all offences.   (10: 12)

So prevalent is this type, in fact, that it serves to express what, if anything, is the central theme of this kind of 'sentence literature'— the antithesis between wisdom and folly or, in its later and specifically Israelite form, between righteousness and sin.

To take another, and final, example of the different ways in which these two-member proverbs are structured, we might look at the comparative type:

> Better is a dry morsel with quiet
> than a house full of feasting with strife   (17: 1)

This too corresponds to an important aspect of the sages' instruction: how to evaluate options and make wise choices. A more emphatic version is what we might call the *a fortiori* type:

> If the poor are hated by their kin;
> how much more are they shunned by their friends!   (19: 7)

or, at a deeper level:

> Sheol and Abaddon lie open before Yahweh,
> how much more human hearts!   (15: 11)

There are other types, but these may serve to illustrate the flexibility of the proverb as a didactic instrument.

The religious dimension

To grasp something of the specifically religious aspect of this aphoristic literature, let us begin by taking another look at how it is presented in the Book of Proverbs. At first sight, it is difficult to detect any rationale for the arrangement either of the proverbs in the two long collections (375 in the first, 133 in the second, not counting 27: 23–7) or the eight compilations (counting 24: 23–34 as an appendix to 22: 17—24: 22) of which the book is composed. If we take another glance at the table of contents laid out above we may detect an *artistic* arrangement of the several parts somewhat in the following manner:

Instruction (1: 8—9: 18)	Instruction (22: 17—24: 34)
Proverbs (10: 1—22: 26)	Proverbs (25–29)

Sayings of Agur (30: 1–14)   Sayings of Lemuel (31: 1–9)
Numerical Sayings (30: 15–33)   Acrostic Poem (31: 10–31)

Whether the arrangement is anything more than formal, however, is difficult to say. Note, however, that the acrostic poem (each line beginning with a letter of the Hebrew alphabet) at the end, which sings the praises of the ideal wife, corresponds to the presentation of the Woman called Wisdom (*ḥokmah*) in the first section. This suggests that the poem at the end has an allegorical or metaphorical as well as a literal meaning, and that the entire book derives its authority from a supramundane wisdom of divine origin. As for the individual proverbial sayings in the two collections, indications of orderly arrangement are few and far between. Some are grouped on the catchword principle (e.g. gold, 25: 11–12), or according to type (e.g. simile, 25: 11–14, 18–20). Sayings contrasting the righteous and the wicked tend to cluster (e.g. 10: 20–32; 11: 4–11; 12: 2–7), but there does not seem to be any overall systematic order in their presentation.

Some progress may, nevertheless, be made along a different line of enquiry. We note that the book contains several examples of two variants of the same saying, sometimes in the same collection. One instance, a particularly graphic one, occurs in one of the two instructions:

> The lazy person says, 'There is a lion in the road!
> There is a lion in the streets!' (26: 13, cf. 22: 13)

—certainly as good an excuse as any for not getting out of bed in the morning. Most of these (e.g. 14: 12 = 16: 25; 18: 8 = 26: 22; 19: 12 = 20: 2) have no particular significance except to remind us that the collections have undergone extensive editing. But there are a few which suggest a deliberate modification made for a specifically religious purpose. Since proverbs are practically impossible to date, more than one explanation of such variants is possible. But it is arguable that this kind of instruction was not, in its original form, particularly religious in character, or at least not Yahwistic. Other aspects of cultural and religious life in Israel were eventually brought into line with Yahwistic orthodoxy, which makes it reasonable to conclude that the same happened to the instruction imparted by sages and scribes. Compare, for example:

> The crucible is for silver, and the furnace is for gold,
> so a person is tested by being praised. (27: 21)

with

> The crucible is for silver, and the furnace is for gold,
> but Yahweh tests the heart. (17: 3)

The former is in accord with the ethos of the old wisdom according to which everyone must pass the test of public approval. The latter introduces a quite different criterion of evaluation which in fact calls the older wisdom into question. Even clearer is the saying which describes the teaching of the sages as a fountain of life (13: 14, cf. 16: 22), when we compare it with the following:

> The fear of Yahweh is a fountain of life,
> so that one may avoid the snares of death. (14: 27)

It seems reasonable to conclude that an early corpus of gnomic material, embodying the kind of prudential, religiously neutral, and sometimes even simply opportunistic ethic found, for example, in Egyptian instructions, has been given a Yahwistic 'baptism'. The difference in attitude between certain proverbs and sets of proverbs will be seen more clearly if we take the example of the acquisition and use of wealth, a subject of great interest to the sages. In some proverbs poverty is simply a misfortune:

> The wealth of the rich is their fortress;
> the poverty of the poor is their ruin. (10: 15, cf. 18: 11)

Others offer advice on how to get rich:

> Wealth hastily gotten will dwindle;
> but those who gather little by little will increase it. (13: 11)

and remind us that money is the best way to make friends and influence people:

> The poor are disliked even by their neighbour;
> but the rich have many friends. (14: 20, cf. 19: 4, 7)

We are also reminded that a little greasing of the palm may at times be the answer to a particular problem:

A bribe is like a magic stone in the eyes of those who give it;
   wherever they turn they prosper. (17: 8)

or

A gift in secret averts anger;
   and a concealed bribe in the bosom, strong wrath. (21: 14)

Informed by a quite different ethos are those proverbs which incul-
cate a basic distrust of wealth:

Riches do not profit in the day of wrath,
   but righteousness delivers from death. (11: 4)

Those who trust in their riches will wither,
   but the righteous will flourish like green leaves. (11: 28)

Even clearer is the condemnation of bribery, especially when used to
pervert the course of justice:

The wicked accept a concealed bribe
   to pervert the ways of justice. (17: 23)

We are reminded of the stipulation in the oldest collection of
Israelite laws, the so-called Covenant Code: 'You shall take no bribe,
for a bribe blinds the officials and subverts the cause of those who
are in the right' (Exod. 23: 8). By the simple substitution of 'wise'
for 'officials' the Deuteronomic law (Deut. 16: 19) has brought the
sapiential tradition of Israel to bear on the administration of justice—
another example of the confluence of the sapiential and legal traditions. In brief, it seems that these variants point to a transformation
of the old international scribal tradition under the influence of the
religion of Yahweh and its representatives.

   This process of adaptation and indigenization can also be detected
in the second instruction in the book (Prov. 22: 17—24: 22) which
has numerous parallels with the Egyptian Instruction of Amen-em-
opet, a high-ranking scribe from about the seventh century BCE. This
work stands out in the corpus of Egyptian didactic writing for its
high moral tone and concern for the powerless, which would certainly help to explain its appeal to a devout Israelite sage. The similarity in tone, in theme, and even at times in language can be seen
in the following example:

> Guard thyself against robbing the oppressed,
> and against overbearing the disabled.   (ch. 2)

> Do not rob the poor because they are poor,
> or crush the afflicted at the gate.   (Prov. 22: 22)

or even more specifically:

> Do not carry off the landmark at the boundaries of the
> arable land,
> nor disturb the position of the measuring cord;
> be not greedy for a cubit of land,
> nor encroach upon the boundaries of a widow . . .
> Guard against encroaching upon the boundaries of the
> fields
> lest a terror carry thee off.   (ch. 6)

> Do not remove the ancient landmark
> that your ancestors set up.   (Prov. 22: 28)

> Do not remove an ancient landmark
> or encroach on the fields of orphans;
> for their redeemer is strong;
> he will plead their cause against you.   (Prov. 23: 10–11)

The adaptation involved recognition of Yahweh as upholder of the moral order (22: 23; 24: 17–18) and the inculcation of the 'fear of Yahweh'—meaning a way of life appropriate to the cult of Yahweh—as the epitome of order and morality (23: 17; 24: 1). It was also to be expected that the ethical teaching contained in the Egyptian instruction should be reinforced by referring to the contrasting fates of the righteous and the wicked (24: 15–16).

The evidence for adaptation and development within the book leads to the conclusion that collections of proverbs expressing the common ethos of the scribal schools were modified and supplemented by religious teachers in the later period of the Judean monarchy or during and after the Babylonian exile. Characteristic features of this more explicitly religious phase are the fear of Yahweh as the epitome of the moral life (e.g. 10: 27), the belief in Yahweh as sustainer of the moral order (e.g. 10: 3), the description of certain kinds of conduct as an 'abomination to Yahweh' (e.g. 11: 1, 20; cf. the 'abomination laws' in Deut. 17: 1 etc.), the use of specifically religious categories such as sin, prayer, and sacrifice, and the contrast, monotonously repeated, between the fate of the righteous and that of the wicked. A further conclusion is that among the devout scribes of this later period the contrast between the righteous and the wicked tends to displace the contrasting portraits of the wise person and the fool in the older wisdom teaching. Since this is the starting point for all later developments, it might be well to examine it more closely before going any further.

The ethic of the sages

The basic assumption of the sapiential tradition in the Near East was that wisdom is a quality of life which can be learned. Hence the emphasis in Proverbs on discipline and education, apparent in the numerous allusions to wise or foolish sons (e.g. 10: 1; 15: 20; 19: 13). Hence also the standard apostrophe 'my son' in the proverbs and instructions, referring to the disciple or student and reminding us that these compendia of proverbial sayings were meant to serve as educational manuals for the young male members of families wealthy enough to launch their sons on lucrative careers in the Judean civil service—maybe no more than one per cent of the population.

The most important item on the curriculum was not theology but decorum and etiquette, and especially the prudent use of speech:

> One who is clever conceals knowledge,
>> but the mind of a fool broadcasts folly.   (12: 23)

> If one gives answer before hearing,
>> it is folly and shame.   (18: 13)

> Do you see someone who is hasty in speech?
>> There is more hope for a fool than for anyone like that.
>>> (29: 20)

This is precisely the kind of injunction which occurs routinely in Egyptian instructions and such Mesopotamian texts as the Words of Ahiqar. Contrasted with the wise person who is cool and temperate in speech, knows the virtues of silence and, in Hamlet's words, is not 'passion's slave', is the 'hot man' who takes no advice, has not acquired the habit of listening and speaks out of season:

> Like a city breached, without walls,
>   is one who lacks self-control.   (25: 28)

It also follows that one must choose one's company with care, for

> Whoever walks with the wise becomes wise,
>   but the companion of fools suffers harm.   (13: 20)

or, as Plutarch put in it his treatise *On the Education of Children*, 'if you live with a lame man you will learn to limp'. The prudent man will also govern his household with firmness and discretion. Family values are all-important, and are to be inculcated by strict training and discipline including corporal punishment. Hard work and husbandry are the keys to success (e.g. Prov. 12: 10–11; 13: 23; 27: 23–7). When going about his business, and especially when away from the home, the prudent and upwardly mobile young male will eschew the company of women and avoid visiting prostitutes. In the presence of higher authority he will assume an appropriate attitude of respect, not speaking out of turn and not being too forward (e.g. 25: 6–7). And he will act in this way not just to avoid the embarrassment of being put in his place but because it is the appropriate thing to do in the circumstances.

It would be easy to criticize this teaching as at best pedestrian and at worst complaisant and ethically insensitive on a whole range of issues. While it frequently enjoins attention to the rights of the poor and disadvantaged, as do the Egyptian instructions, it simply takes for granted a hierarchical and feudal society in which advancement depends upon wealth and influence in high places. Its consistently derogatory and petulant attitude to women (e.g. 19: 13; 21: 9, 19; 25: 24; 27: 15–16) is by no means peculiar to Israel, but that will do little to alleviate the distasteful impression which it conveys. (It reaches the nadir of irrationality in Ben Sira's statement that 'better is the wickedness of a man than a woman who does good', Ecclus. 42: 14). We have to remind ourselves that, with the exception of the advice of the queen mother to Lemuel (31: 1–9), this is literature written by and for men. So that even where women are praised it will not always seem to us to be for the right reasons—witness the *petit bourgeois* portrait of the 'valiant woman' or the 'woman of substance' with its catalogue of managerial skills (31: 10–31). Its educational theory, if we may call it that, has too much of the 'spare the rod, spoil the child' approach to gain wide endorsement today (e.g. 10: 13; 13: 24; 19: 18; 22: 15; 29: 15). And, in general, much of it seems to be aimed at getting on, or sometimes just getting by, in life.

While such a negative criticism would certainly hold for a good part of the material we are surveying, enough of the traditional mores which sustained the kinship system has been incorporated in it to allow us to consider its positive aspects. Its inculcation of the virtues of truth, honesty, and self-control in public life has nothing to fear from comparison with standards which have come to be accepted, or tolerated, in our contemporary societies. In its search for order behind the apparent chaos of experience, its endeavour to teach how to discriminate between options and make reasonable choices, its delineation of human types, it laid the basis for a genuine social ethic applicable outside the class to which it was first addressed. As such, its contribution to public life in Israel has a highly distinctive quality which should not be ignored.

The instruction

So far we have dealt almost exclusively with the proverb as a didactic instrument used by teachers and sages. The reason is that the proverb was taken to be the basic unit of instruction in the schools, and therefore one of the principal activities of teachers such as Qoheleth was the collecting, arranging, and evaluating of proverbs (Eccles. 12: 9). But the sages used a wide variety of literary forms apart from the proverb, each one of which would require careful and detailed treatment. We will take a brief look at some of the more important of these, paying special attention to their use as didactic tools and the connections which can be shown to exist between them.

From ancient Egypt several complete or fragmentary examples of the instruction have survived covering a vast period of time with relatively little evidence of development. Purporting to be advice from a pharaoh in his declining years to the crown prince (e.g. the Instruction of Meri-ka-re), or from a vizier to his son who is to succeed him in office (e.g. Ptah-hotep in the third millennium BCE), or by a lower-echelon administrator to his son (e.g. Amen-em-opet), these admonitions are cast in direct address, make frequent use of the imperative, and provide motivation for the faithful implementation of the precepts. Remarkably stable as it is, this genre was favoured by moralists and philosophers in Late Antiquity, flourished in the Middle Ages, and passed into modern European literature as a well-known literary convention, e.g. in the plays of Shakespeare. One can get a good idea of the typical content and conventions of such admonitory addresses by reading the speech of Polonius to Hamlet as the latter was preparing to embark for England.

This type of instruction was taken over by Israelite sages into their curriculum, how soon we do not know, and continued in use down into the Second Temple. In Proverbs the section entitled 'Sayings of Lemuel' (31: 1–9) approximates most closely to the Egyptian type in that it purports to be a charge delivered by the queen mother to her son who is either preparing to reign or has just begun to do so. It is therefore presented explicitly as a 'mirror for princes' and contains the usual admonitions to avoid sexual irregularity, drunkenness, and injustice. As noted earlier, another section (22: 17—24: 22) appears to be modelled on the Egyptian Instruction of Amen-em-opet and, like the latter, is divided into thirty units. These, however, are much shorter than the chapters of the Egyptian text, usually running to no more than four lines. The structure is simple: an admonition in the imperative in the first couplet is followed by appropriate motivation in the second:

> Do not rob the poor because they are poor,
>   or crush the afflicted at the gate;
> for Yahweh pleads their cause
>   and despoils of life those who despoil them.   (22: 22–3)

In a later chapter we shall see that this pattern—imperative or prohibitive accompanied by motivation—occurs in the Decalogue and in other types of legal enactment, thus providing a further indication of the link between legal and sapiential–didactic genres. There are also longer units in this 'Egyptian' instruction in which the imperative–motivation unit has dissolved into something rather different: either a depiction of a particular human type (e.g. the liar, the sluggard) or a graphic description of the consequences of acting in a certain way. Take drunkenness, for example:

> Who has woe? Who has sorrow?
>   Who has strife? Who has complaining?
> Who has wounds without cause?
>   Who has redness of eyes?
> Those who linger late over wine,
>   those who keep trying mixed wines.
> Do not look at wine when it is red,
>   when it sparkles in the cup and goes down smoothly.
> At the last it bites like a serpent,
>   and stings like an adder.
> Your eyes will see strange things,
>   and your mind utter perverse things.
> You will be like one who lies down in the midst of the sea,
>   like one who lies on the top of a mast.
> 'They struck me,' you will say, 'but I was not hurt;
>   they beat me, but I did not feel it.
> When shall I awake?
>   I will seek another drink.' (23: 29–35)

Even in its most compressed form, the instruction differs from the typical proverb in its addiction to the imperative. There are, nevertheless, significant links between the instruction and the proverb which can best be illustrated by an example. The proverbial aphorism, 'pride comes before a fall', simply states compendiously a causal connection on the basis of many individual observations. The instructional counterpart, using the imperative, would be something like, 'know your place' or 'don't step out of line'. The proverbial form occurs in the Solomonic collections:

> When pride comes, then comes disgrace;
>   but wisdom is with the humble. (11: 2)

or, alternatively,

> Pride goes before destruction,
>   and a haughty spirit before a fall. (16: 18)

In the second Solomonic collection the same point is made in the form characteristic of the instruction:

> Do not put yourself forward in the king's presence
>   or stand in the place of the great;

> for it is better to be told, 'Come up here,'
> than to be put lower in the presence of a noble.   (25: 6–7)

This will bring to mind the gospel passage (Luke 14: 7–11) which is presented as a parable of Jesus but is in fact an instruction rounded off with a proverbial saying. It may be set out as follows:

From exaltation to humiliation
When you are invited by someone to a wedding banquet, do not sit down at the place of honour, in case someone more distinguished than you has been invited by your host; and the host who invited both of you may come and say to you, 'Give this person your place,' and then in disgrace you would start to take the lowest place.

From humiliation to exaltation
But when you are invited, go and sit down at the lowest place, so that when your host comes, he may say to you, 'Friend, move up higher'; then you will be honoured in the presence of all who sit at the table with you.

Paradox and reversal
For all who exalt themselves will be humbled, and those who humble themselves will be exalted.

We see how the brief instruction in Proverbs, itself an expanded version of an even briefer proverb, has here been expanded into two contrasting units to allow for the kind of paradoxical saying which seems to have been characteristic of the teaching of Jesus (see Mark 8: 36–7; 10: 31; Luke 17: 33).

This facility in transposing the same basic message from one genre to another can be observed in several gospel sayings. To take only one further example, the proverbial saying, 'anyone who tends a fig tree will eat its fruit' (Prov. 27: 18), appears to have suggested the particular form of an oracle of judgement in Jeremiah (8: 13) where Yahweh comes to harvest figs from his fig tree—meaning Israel—and finds none. In the gospels the same figure appears both in the form of a parable (Luke 13: 6–9) and as the prophetic–symbolic action of the cursing of the barren fig tree (Matt. 21: 18–22).

Returning once again to Proverbs, we note that the first section also contains examples of the instruction, here too of the fairly short type introduced by the conventional apostrophe 'my son . . .'. Many of these have been expanded in different ways, for example, with rhetorical questions (e.g. 6: 27–8), vivid description (e.g. 7: 6–23), autobiographical reflections (4: 4–9), or perorations (7: 24–7). The kind of advice given is not significantly different from that of the Egyptian sages: avoidance of bad company and of prostitutes, keeping the passions under control, performance of duties to the neighbour and to God. The section also contains portraits of the sluggard, the devious character, the seductive prostitute, of a kind encountered in cautionary tales from all ages. The most remarkable feature, however, is the public address of Wisdom to the foolish and uninstructed (1: 20–33; 8: 1–31; 9: 1–6). Because of its importance for later developments, this will call for separate treatment in a subsequent chapter.

Acrostics, numerical sayings, riddles

Among the principal literary forms used by the sages, then, were the proverb and the instruction, and it is these which make up the bulk of the material in the Book of Proverbs. But effective teaching calls for a variety of techniques whether to help the memory, arouse curiosity, or stimulate the mind to make certain associations or draw conclusions from stated premisses. *Acrostic compositions*, in which each line begins with a letter of the Hebrew alphabet in correct sequence, facilitated memorizing and perhaps, in addition, gave their authors the satisfying sense of making an all-inclusive statement. Though not conducive to a high level of poetic expression, as one may see from the poem about the good wife at the end of Proverbs (31: 10–31), they occur with some frequency in liturgical hymns (e.g. Pss. 9–10; 111–12; 145; Lam. 1–4). Better attested is the *numerical saying* which announces a specific number of items and then goes on to enumerate them. In some respects this type of saying resembles the list or onomasticon, a familiar feature in the Egyptian and Sumero-Akkadian scribal traditions, which served to classify and order the phenomena of nature and therefore could be used in teaching subjects such as geography, zoology, and botany. While such educational material has not come down to us from Israel of the biblical period, something of the method is reflected in the tradition of

Solomon's encyclopaedic wisdom, his classification of flora and fauna, alluded to earlier.

The examples of the genre in Proverbs are somewhat different in that the emphasis is really on human conduct even when they deal in what used to be called 'natural history'. Thus, the four small but wise creatures in Proverbs 30: 24–8 are chosen as apt to teach valuable lessons in social living:

> Four things on earth are small,
>   yet they are exceedingly wise:
> the ants are a people without strength,
>   yet they provide their food in the summer;
> the badgers are a people without power,
>   yet they make their homes in the rocks;
> the locusts have no king,
>   yet all of them march in rank;
> the lizard can be grasped in the hand,
>   yet it is found in kings' palaces.

A negative lesson can also be learned from the leech and its suckers, if that is the meaning of the obscure term in Proverbs 30: 15. Arrangement in numerical sequence has an obviously mnemonic function and has been used to teach children since time immemorial. One thinks of the children's song at the end of the Passover Seder:

> Who knows one? I know one.
> One is our God in heaven and on earth.
> Who knows two? I know two.
> Two are the tablets of the covenant;
> One is our God in heaven and on earth.

—and so on in progressive and cumulative sequence up to the thirteen attributes of God. Many other examples of the use of this technique in secular instruction and religious catechesis could be given. The arrangements of laws in sets of ten (to be counted on the ten fingers?) may also have had the same mnemonic function.

A special kind of numerical saying is the type in which two numbers, one higher than the other, occur; we could call it the progressive numerical saying. Starting from the common practice of indicating approximation by numbers in sequence ('two or three'), this type is stylized according to the verse parallelism characteristic of Hebrew poetry. Together with other literary conventions, it appears to have been taken over from Canaanite poetics, as the following example from the Ugaritic Baal-cycle suggests:

> Two sacrifices Baal hates,
>   three, the Rider on the Clouds:
> a sacrifice of shame,
> a sacrifice of meanness,
>   and a sacrifice of the lewdness of handmaids

—referring, no doubt, to irregularities and abuses in the practice of the sacrificial cult the precise nature of which is no longer apparent. With this we may compare Proverbs 6: 16–19:

> There are six things that Yahweh hates,
>   seven which are an abomination to him:
> haughty eyes, a lying tongue,
>   and hands that shed innocent blood,
> a heart that devises wicked plans,
>   feet that hurry to run to evil,
> a lying witness who testifies falsely,
>   and one who sows discord in a family.

Most of our examples are concentrated in the seventh section of the book (Prov. 30: 10–33) and in Ben Sira. Almost all of the combinations between one–two (Ps. 62: 11–12; Job 33: 14) and nine–ten (Ecclus. 25: 7) are attested, the majority of them at the lower end. While the intent is clearly mnemonic, some of them have a riddle-like quality, as if to tease the mind into considering realities below the level of everyday observation. While not entirely characteristic of the genre, the following example seems to be of this kind:

> Three things are too wonderful for me;
>   four I do not understand:
> the way of an eagle in the sky,
>   the way of a snake on a rock,
> the way of a ship on the high seas,
>   and the way of a man with a girl.   (Prov. 30: 18–19)

In this instance the sequence has the effect of stressing the fourth 'way', in the sense that the mysterious element in the first three is where one has to look for the key, the clue to the meaning. In other words, the common element in the first three, a mysterious form of propulsion, leads into a consideration of the deep mystery of sexual attraction. For the Hebrew reader the point would have been reinforced by a cunning play on words, since the word *derek* (way) also has a sexual connotation—as, for example, in Proverbs 31: 3, where 'ways' is parallel with 'virility'.

It will be inevitable to think of a connection of some sort between this kind of saying and the *riddle* which also, not uncommonly, deals with sexual matters. While no collection of Hebrew riddles has survived, it is explicitly stated that their composition and solution fell within the competence of the sages (Prov. 1: 6). In this respect, as in others, Solomon was the model sage. We hear of the Queen of Sheba (or Saba) coming to test him with riddles, and it is quite conceivable that a collection of riddles originally stood at this point in the narrative. In the Midrash she is transformed into the demon Lilith, and her riddles, like those of the Sphinx, are lethal: you get it right or you die. Josephus too records contests of this kind between Solomon and foreign sages (*Antiquities* 8: 146–9), and 1 Esdras: 3–4 has the famous riddle-like story of the dispute at the court of Darius as to which was strongest, wine, kings, or women, all three being capped by truth. Riddles were used in Israel, as in other cultures, for many purposes. The Hebrew term (*hidah*) is used for certain liturgical compositions (Pss. 49: 5; 78: 2) and for the dark and sometimes ambiguous utterances of a prophet (Num. 12: 8; Ezek. 17: 2; Hab. 2: 6). In both cases there is the sense that, at its deepest levels, human existence inevitably has a riddle-like quality about it.

At the level of popular usage the riddle was, of course, a means of entertainment, being an especially popular feature at banquets. The riddling that went on at Samson's wedding feast is the only example which has come down to us, but provides a good instance of both content and form. It was a genuine contest, with a considerable wager at stake, the riddles being propounded in a thinly concealed atmosphere of hostility and menace. Samson's initial riddle:

> Out of the eater came something to eat;
> Out of the strong came something sweet.   (Judg. 14: 14)

is also typical in that, like several of the Anglo-Saxon riddles, the surface meaning served to disguise a deeper meaning, often of a sexual nature. In the hands of the sages this universally popular form of diversion came to serve a didactic purpose, presenting the well-known in new ways, redefining the familiar, stretching and sharpening the mind of the student.

The *dialogue*, *debate*, or *dispute* could also serve as a medium of instruction, especially for the formulation and solution of problems of a speculative nature. Since the biblical examples of Job and of Abraham's dialogue with God over the fate of Sodom (Gen. 18) take us well beyond any scholastic curriculum, they should be classified as speculative rather than didactic wisdom, and as such they will be considered in a subsequent chapter. Confessional and autobiographical passages, generally spoken under an assumed identity, belong to the same class. Their best representatives are the Egyptian instructions and the 'royal testament' of Qoheleth. Other non-narrative genres sometimes listed as sapiential, the didactic poem for example, simply illustrate the fact that the sages could make use of practically any literary form when it served their purpose to do so.

Sapiential narrative

We are on much less certain ground when we go on to ask what use the sages made of narrative for didactic purposes. The *parable* is an obvious place to start, but presents us at once with a problem of definition. Apart from the fact that there is no Hebrew term which clearly designates this genre as distinct from the proverb, our perception of what a parable is and how it works tends to be determined by the gospel parables which happen to be the best known but may not be the most typical. A satisfactory solution to this problem would require a broad comparative study which cannot be undertaken here. Parables attributed to Jesus, and to other Jewish sages of Late Antiquity, at least demonstrate that there is an affinity between the proverb and the parable similar to that between the proverb and the instruction which we noted earlier. Thus, the gospel parables which compare the Kingdom of Heaven to a field, a net, or a batch of yeast, may be read as narrative parallels to the simile-proverbs discussed earlier in this chapter. And, in general, the vivid and concrete language of Hebrew aphorisms would make it relatively easy to develop their narrative nucleus in parabolic form. To take an example at random:

> Like somebody who takes a passing dog by the ears
> is one who meddles in the quarrel of another. (Prov. 26: 17)

This proverbial saying could, without much difficulty, be transposed into a brief and vivid parable.

As far as we can judge from the surviving literature, the sages of Israel seem to have made relatively little use of the parable for purposes of instruction. Perhaps the best known in the Hebrew Bible is the parable of the pet lamb:

There were two men in a certain city, the one rich and the other poor. The rich man had very many flocks and herds; but the poor man had nothing but one little ewe lamb, which he had bought. He brought it up, and it grew up with him and with his children; it used to eat of his meagre fare, and drink from his cup, and lie in his bosom, and it was like a daughter to him. Now there came a traveller to the rich man, and he was loath to take one of his own flock or herd to prepare for the wayfarer who had come to him, but he took the poor man's lamb and prepared that for the guest who had come to him. (2 Sam. 12: 1–4)

The story is told by the prophet Nathan to David after the latter had committed adultery with Bathsheba and murdered her husband, but it is doubtful whether it is native to this narrative context: Bathsheba was Uriah's wife not his daughter, she was destined for David himself not a visiting guest, and it was Uriah not Bathsheba who ended up dead. It nevertheless illustrates very well the essential characteristics of the parable. It is a brief narrative with an overt meaning concealing a meaning at a different level, and its purpose is to involve the reader. So well does this particular example work that David, forgetful of his own situation and of the fictional nature of the narrative, passes sentence of death on himself:

David's anger was greatly kindled against the man, He said to Nathan, 'as Yahweh lives, the man who has done this deserves to die'. (12: 5)

The story which the wise woman of Tekoa told David about her two sons one of whom, having killed the other, is in immediate danger of death (2 Sam. 14: 4–7), is a skilful fictionalization of the situation in David's family, but no parable. The same must be said of the prophet's story, told to king Ahab, about losing a prisoner-of-war (1 Kgs. 20: 35–43). Other passages which are sometimes adduced as examples are the unproductive vineyard (Isa. 5: 1–2) and the sensible farmer (28: 23–6). While they share with many of the parables of Jesus the scenario of the countryside, they are not really narrative and occur, significantly, in a prophetic book.

More clearly didactic in purpose is the *fable*, understood as a short story featuring animals or inanimate things as actors, which is designed to teach a lesson or make a point. The animal fable, of the kind favoured by Aesop, seems to have been very popular among the Sumerians as far back as the third millennium BCE. Since the juxtaposition of animal and human types easily brings into play both the comic and the cruel, the fable also lends itself to satire. An extremely brief example is the answer sent by a king of Israel in the early eighth century BCE to a king of Judah who had challenged him to do battle:

A thorn bush on Lebanon sent to a cedar on Lebanon, saying, 'Give your daughter to my son for a wife'; but a wild beast of Lebanon passed by and trampled down the thorn bush. (2 Kgs. 14: 9)

More extended in length is the fable of the convocation of trees which assembled to choose a king and which ended with the bramble putting himself forward successfully for election (Judg. 9: 7–15). In its present context it serves as a savagely effective satire on the pretensions of the usurper Abimelech and perhaps also on monarchy in general.

While these are the only examples of the fable in the Hebrew Bible, we have no reason to doubt that the genre was popular in ancient Israel and in use in the schools. Animal and plant fables occur in the teaching of the legendary Ahiqar known to the Jewish colony which settled at Elephantine in the Upper Nile in the fifth century BCE. Fables were also used to teach natural history in Mesopotamia, to judge by extant examples such as the Babylonian 'Dispute between the Tamarisk and the Date Palm'. No such example has, however, survived from ancient Israel.

Scholars have been debating for a long time as to whether certain longer narratives in the Hebrew Bible and the Apocrypha can be placed within the 'wisdom movement' or have at least been subjected to 'wisdom influences'. What this presumably means is that in certain cases the *primary* intent in composing a narrative was to make a point or teach a lesson rather than, for example, to record history or entertain. Unfortunately, this is not always possible to determine with a reasonable degree of probability. Since all composers of biblical narrative of any kind were trained in the same scribal conventions, it will not be surprising to find an overlap in theme and vocabulary with the core 'wisdom' books (Proverbs, Job, Ecclesiastes). What, however, remains to be determined is whether the *primary* intent of the writer is didactic and discursive or something quite different.

In the previous chapter we touched briefly on the court history dealing with the succession to David's throne (2 Sam. 11–20; 1 Kgs. 1–2) and noted that it embodies themes and language characteristic of the sages. This has led some few scholars to read it as essentially historical fiction, composed long after the time of the United Monarchy as a kind of extended political parable. Others, however, find this difficult to reconcile with the detailed and plausible description of persons and situations and the intent to legitimate Solomon's claim to the succession. A more convincing case can be made for the story of the Garden of Eden (Gen. 2: 4—3: 24) as a deep and subtle symbolic narrative. Its learned use of mythological themes, skilful dialogue and profound exploration of the limits of human resources suggest a sapiential origin. We note in passing that mythological themes abound in the writings which are explicitly sapiential: the first man (Job 15: 7–8), the tree of life (Prov. 3: 18), the rebellion of heavenly beings (Job 4: 18; 15: 15; 25: 5), monsters of the deep (e.g. Job 3: 8; 7: 12; 9: 13) and many others. It is therefore by no means implausible that the sages of Israel took over well-known mythic narrative themes for their own purposes.

Since the principal milieu of the scribes and sages in early Israel was the court, it is not surprising that several narratives which bear their imprint have a court setting. The obvious example is the succession history, discussed earlier, which features a contest of sages and pits the professional wisdom of Ahithophel against a providence that guides Solomon to the throne against all human odds. Less obvious, though no less suggestive, is the story of Joseph in Genesis

(37–50). The novelistic character of this narrative stands out quite clearly in contrast to stories about earlier ancestors, Abraham, Isaac, and Jacob, and it differs from them in other significant respects as well. The deeper levels of meaning are revealed not through visions and theophanies but in dreams—those of Joseph himself (37: 5–11), the pharaoh (41: 1–8), and his servants (40: 5–19). Joseph rises to prominence at the Egyptian court because he is recognized to be 'a man discreet and wise' (41: 33, 39), and his wisdom includes skill in dream interpretation and divination (41: 15; 44: 15). This wisdom is a divine gift, a reward for his fidelity (39: 2–3, 21–3) demonstrated in his rejection of a married woman's advances (39: 6–18). As in the court history of David, the action is controlled from beginning to end by a hidden providence. As Joseph explains to his brothers:

Even though you intended to do harm to me, God intended it for good, in order to preserve a numerous people, as he is doing today. (Gen. 50: 20)

There has been much inconclusive and generally unhelpful discussion as to whether this prose masterpiece is 'sapiential' or not. What we can say is that it is closer to historical fiction than straightforward history-writing, and it was written both as entertainment and as moral instruction. Moreover, the entire story breathes the atmosphere of the sages and bears comparison with other biblical narratives in which similar themes appear, e.g. the court tales in Daniel 1–6 which we shall consider in Chapter 6.

Much of the action in Esther, another historical novel or novelette, also takes place at court, this time during the Persian period (6th to 4th century BCE). The principal characters are presented in idealized and paradigmatic rather than realistic fashion. Esther (Hadassah) herself is a woman of beauty, wisdom, and courage; Mordecai, her cousin and guardian, is a wise and prudent counsellor; Haman, descendant of the hated Agag and the Amalekites, is the archetypal enemy of the Jewish people; Ahasuerus (Xerxes I) is the same kind of witless and befuddled tyrant as the pharaoh of the Egyptian oppression and Holofernes in Judith. The account of Haman's undoing, ending with his death on the gibbet which he had prepared for Mordecai, provides a perfect illustration of the sages' teaching on retribution. So the author has certainly made use of procedures and themes familiar to the teachers of wisdom. Since, however, the story in its present form is meant to explain the origins of the festival of Purim, it can hardly be described as didactic in the sense of teaching important lessons for the conduct of life. The militantly nationalistic tone is also unparalleled in other sapiential compositions known to us and would lead us to look elsewhere for its origins.

Much of the same problem—that of genre or category—confronts us in reading Judith, one of the additional books of the Greek Bible, and here too only a brief comment will be possible. The story relates how the Assyrian king Nebuchadnezzar sent his general Holofernes on a punitive expedition against his rebellious subjects in Phoenicia and Palestine. Israel being the only province to resist, Holofernes took counsel with his vassals and was advised by Achior, the Ammonite leader, that the Jews were invincible as long as they took care to observe their laws. Disregarding this advice, he laid siege to Bethulia, a town in the Central Highlands which blocked his advances on Jerusalem. After cutting off the town's water supply, Holofernes reduced the inhabitants to such straits that they demanded of Uzziah their leader that he capitulate. At this point Judith, a wealthy and devout widow, prevailed upon Uzziah to allow her to execute a cunningly devised plan to seduce the Assyrian general, assassinate him, and thus throw his entire army into disarray. The plan succeeded, and the story comes to a climax of gothic horror with Judith pulling the general's severed head from her lunch bag and showing it to her compatriots:

Then she pulled the head out of the bag and showed it to them, and said, 'See here, the head of Holofernes, the commander of the Assyrian army, and here is the canopy beneath which he lay in his drunken stupour. Yahweh has struck him down by the hand of a woman.'

(Judith. 13: 15)

Those who argue that this narrative is sapiential or didactic can point to the portrayal of Judith as a model of wisdom (8: 29; 11: 20–3) combined with piety; indeed, since Judith means 'Jewess', as *the* model of Israelite womanhood. While this is correct as far as it goes, it does not help very much in determining with any precision what the story is really about. That the Babylonian Nebuchadnezzar is described as king of the Assyrians will remind us of his role in the court tales in Daniel 1–6 where he stands for Antiochus IV, ruler of the Syrian kingdom of the Seleucids. This will be confirmed by references in Judith to the cult of the divinized king (3: 8; 6: 2), the plundering and destruction of temples (3: 8; 4: 1–2, etc.), the fact that Israel alone resisted the tyrant (3–4)) and the similarity between the fate of Holofernes and that of the Seleucid general Nicanor (1 Macc. 7: 43–50). Following the lead of these different clues scattered throughout the book, we should read it as a celebration of the Maccabean triumph written not long after Daniel. Judith herself, then, would embody the kind of assiduous, proto-Pharisaic piety illustrated in Daniel. She prays at the proper times (11: 17; 13: 3), fasts (8: 6), observes sabbath (10: 2), the food laws (12: 2–4), tithing and first-fruits (11: 12–15), together with the prescribed ritual ablutions (12: 7–9). In acting thus she demonstrates a God-given wisdom which enables her to save her people. If this means that the book is sapiential or didactic, we would probably have to say the same of almost all the religious narrative literature which has survived from the Graeco-Roman period. By that time, in fact, the sapiential tradition was fully assimilated to Torah piety.

We conclude that the further we get away from the basic instruments of instruction in the scribal schools the less useful is the term 'sapiential' as a descriptive label. This is true of Judith and also of Tobit, another book in the Greek Bible which deals with exemplary conduct and its reward. But even without these borderline cases, enough has been said to establish the remarkable range and versatility of the instruction which the sages of Israel offered.

3

God and the Moral Order

The link between act and consequence

One of the ways in which the sages of Israel, and of the ancient world in general, attempted to make sense of human existence was to postulate an intrinsic connection between act and consequence and thereby lay the basis for a morally significant life. The observation that pride leads to disaster (e.g. Prov. 11: 2; 16: 18; 18: 12), or that laziness generally leads to poverty (e.g. Prov. 10: 4; 20: 13; 21: 25), made on the basis of experience, was intended to suggest obvious consequences for the moral life. While this kind of teaching does not amount to a 'doctrine of retribution', it can too easily be applied in doctrinaire fashion and be made to serve as an instrument of moral evaluation. We are all familiar with the point of view that the poor owe their condition to laziness; a conclusion which is true in some instances but inadequate as a general explanation of poverty.

One result of the assimilation of this 'old wisdom' to the specifically religious content of Israel's life as a community was that the act–consequence link gave rise to serious theological problems. Faith in Yahweh entailed the conviction that he presided over and validated the moral order as lord and judge of his people. The intrinsic connection between human deed and its consequences was not thereby abandoned, but the religious dimension made it easier to think in terms of reward and punishment flowing from the divine administration of justice. This can be seen in Solomon's prayer at the dedication of the temple, a passage generally attributed to a Deuteronomic author of the late monarchy or exilic age:

If someone sins against a neighbour and is given an oath to swear . . . then hear in heaven, and act, and judge your servants, condemning the guilty by bringing their conduct on their own head, and vindicating the righteous by rewarding them according to their righteousness.

(1 Kgs. 8: 31–2)

The implication is that good and bad actions are not always seen to have their appropriate consequences, and that therefore the moral order—in this case respect for oaths—demands the intervention of God as judge. It followed that any threat to the moral order risked calling into question either the power or the justice of God.

These implications are apparent in the religiously inspired aphorisms of the two large collections in Proverbs. The idea of an *intrinsic* link between act and consequence is still detectable—for example, in proverbs which speak of sowing and reaping (26: 27; 28: 10)—but the monotonous contrast between the fate of the righteous and that of the wicked is based on specifically religious premisses. Expressions such as the following could hardly arise out of observation and experience alone:

> No harm happens to the righteous,
>> but the wicked are filled with trouble.   (12: 21)

or

> The righteous have enough to satisfy their appetite,
>> but the belly of the wicked is empty.   (13: 25)

Even less could the contention that the wicked come to an untimely end while the righteous live out their days (e.g. Prov. 10: 27). The same view is maintained in the more developed and speculative teaching in Proverbs 1–9, where the motive-clauses frequently attached to the instructions suggest that religious observance ('the fear of Yahweh') is rewarded with long life and well-being (e.g. 3: 1–2, 9–10). Since the language of prayer in Israel addresses God as all-powerful ruler and judge, we would expect to find something like the same point of view in Psalms which, like Proverbs, is a compilation dating in its final form to the late Second Temple period. The first psalm recapitulates an important aspect of scribal piety by contrasting the fate of the wicked with that of the righteous. It concludes:

> For Yahweh watches over the way of the righteous,
>> but the way of the wicked will perish.

Nor is this the only instance of affinity with the wisdom of the scribes. Two other compositions—Psalms. 49 and 78—are presented as proverbial discourse and riddle and deal, in different ways, with the mystery of evil and its consequences. Among psalms composed in the acrostic form—discussed briefly in the previous chapter—we also find this contrast between religious observance and impiety (e.g. Ps. 119). The frequent prayer for vengeance on the wicked, unpalatable as it may be to modern sensitivities, is motivated by the absolute theological necessity for the divine justice to be seen and acknowledged (e.g. Ps. 58). Many of the psalms of individual lamentation presuppose that sickness and other ills are the direct consequence of divine judgement following on sin, even inadvertent sin (e.g. Ps. 90: 7–8). In some of these hymns a morally rational world-view, in which virtue is always rewarded and wickedness always punished, is maintained in defiance of experience:

> I have been young, and now am old,
>> yet I have not seen the righteous forsaken
>> or their children begging bread.   (Ps. 37: 25)

A similar claim would be made by Job's friends in an effort to get him to confess to wrongdoing in some way commensurate with his sufferings and thus maintain the traditional rationale of evil. It testifies to the absolute need to make sense of the world in moral terms and of God's relation to it.

This way of reasoning was by no means peculiar to Israel. It was part of the common theology of the ancient Near East according to which evil was attributed to the anger of a deity resulting from sin, even inadvertent sin. It was not necessary, either, for the effect of sin to be felt at once. On the contrary, the interval between act and consequence could cover many years or even generations. A prayer of Mursilis II, Hittite king of the fourteenth century BCE, was occasioned by a plague which was ravaging the land. On consulting an oracle, the king discovered the cause to be the violation of a treaty with the Egyptians during the previous reign, that of his father. This brought on the anger of Teshub, the Hittite storm-god whose name had been invoked in the treaty, after the lapse of a generation. A rather similar situation occurred with a three-year famine at the beginning of David's reign. David consulted an oracle and discovered that what caused the disaster was Saul's violation of his treaty oath with the Gibeonites several years earlier. The matter was then resolved with the ritual killing of seven of Saul's descendants (2 Sam. 21: 1–14).

The same principle is in evidence in the history of David's family to which we have alluded more than once in the previous chapters. The death of the nameless child born of David's illicit union with Bathsheba is attributed directly to the anger of Yahweh: 'the thing that David had done displeased Yahweh . . . and Yahweh struck the child that Uriah's wife bore to David, and it became very ill' (2 Sam. 11: 27; 12: 15). The ruinous fratricidal strife which broke out among his remaining sons is traced to the same source, as revealed to him in advance by Nathan the seer: 'the sword shall never depart from your house, for you have despised me, and have taken the wife of Uriah the Hittite to be your wife' (2 Sam. 12: 10). This principle of theological causality can be illustrated from any number of incidents in biblical narratives, beginning with the so-called Primeval History (Gen. 1–11) where it is worked out with the help of mythological themes in the broader context of the history of the human family as a whole.

In the prophetic writings the link between sin and punishment—the latter in the form of political disaster—is the more prominent in that the prophets make extensive use of the political analogy of covenant with its associations of overlordship, binding obligations reinforced by curses, and the direct communication of the sovereign's will. If questioned, a prophet such as Amos or Jeremiah might well have agreed that sin brings about its own effect on the sinner by virtue of its own inner dynamic. But this would not be seen as incompatible with the direct judicial intervention of God in the life of the individual and the state. The pattern can be seen in the condemnation of Saul by Samuel, presented as a model of prophetic opposition to the monarchy (1 Sam. 15, cf. 13: 7–15). Though Saul's decision to spare Agag seems positively meritorious to the modern reader, it was condemned by Samuel as a violation of the ban leading to divine rejection and consequent fall from power. Typically, the Chronicler, writing several centuries later, states the lesson explicitly:

So Saul died for his unfaithfulness; he was unfaithful to Yahweh in that he did not keep the command of Yahweh; moreover he had consulted a medium, seeking guidance, and did not seek guidance from Yahweh. Therefore Yahweh put him to death, and turned the kingdom over to David, son of Jesse. (1 Chr. 10: 13-14)

Later still, Josephus will retell the story of Saul as a flawed hero in the manner of Greek tragedy, his final *peripateia* or change of fortune occurring when he conjured up Samuel's ghost (*Antiquities* 6: 45-378).

For the prophets, then, political disaster was the result of divine punishment incurred on account of sin, the more severe in the case of Israel because of the special relationship which bound her to Yahweh (e.g. Amos 3: 2, 14). Indeed, this correlation between human action and divine reaction—whether described as rewarding and punishing, or remembering and forgetting, or in some other way—provided the prophets with the key to deciphering the course of history and projecting the future.

If any part of the Hebrew Bible may be said to contain a *doctrine* of retribution, it would be Deuteronomy. While much about the origins of the book and the law or programme it contains is obscure, and will probably remain so, it would be widely accepted that it corresponds in some way to a sporadic movement of social and cultic reform throughout the history of the Kingdom of Judah which came to a head some years into the reign of Josiah, the last reforming king of Judah (640–609 BCE). It also provides us with the first clear evidence for the administration and interpretation of a law book by the scribal classes. While a more thorough discussion of this book must be postponed to the following chapter, we note in the meantime that the language of teaching and learning occurs often in the book, and that Yahweh is often represented in it as a teacher who disciplines his people by word of mouth (Deut. 4: 36) and through the vicissitudes of history (8: 5). Israel's trials in the wilderness are viewed as a necessary preparation for life in the land (8: 2, 16), and even false prophecy can serve as a kind of testing (13: 3). Deuteronomy abounds in the kind of moralizing and educational language associated with the sages. Exhortations to keep the law are routinely reinforced by motivation clauses of the kind we noted earlier in Proverbs: keep the law and you will live long in the land; neglect it and you will end up in exile (4: 1, 25-7, 40, etc.).

An identical perspective dominates the history of the kingdoms, the final edition of which dates from the exilic period and the author or authors of which belonged to the Deuteronomic school. The pattern is established right from the beginning. Military success against the Canaanites depends on observance of the law (Jos. 1: 8). The history of Israel's heroic age preceding the monarchy is organized according to the same principle: the Israelites lapse into apostasy thus provoking Yahweh to anger; this brings on military disaster which in its turn induces a change of heart; Yahweh sends a military leader to save them in response to their plea for assistance; after the death of the leader they lapse once more into apostasy, and the process is repeated (Judg. 2: 11–23, etc.). During the monarchy the political success of rulers and dynasties is contingent on their religious fidelity. The collapse of the Northern Kingdom results from the setting up of a separatist cult by Jeroboam and the sins of the Omrid dynasty (2 Kgs. 17: 21; cf. Mic. 6: 16). The fall of Jerusalem can be traced back to the apostasy of Manasseh who died more than half a century earlier (2 Kgs. 21: 10–15; 23: 26–7; 24: 3–4). From beginning to end the history is dominated by this law of moral causality which also serves to explain and justify the divine judgement which overtook the nation and its rulers.

Political disaster and religious crisis

In any society a religion, or its equivalent, provides a basic orientation and cohesive world-view which is usually strong enough to survive the occasional inevitable discrepancy between theory and experience. Naturally, there will always be individuals whose experience will lead them to question, and sometimes even to reject, the account of reality offered by the religion. It is therefore not surprising that several psalms quote the wicked as, in effect, denying the existence of God, which, in that historical context, means denying the possibility of divine intervention in their affairs:

> In the pride of their countenance the wicked say, 'God
>   will not seek it out,'
>   all their thoughts are, 'There is no God,'   (10: 4)

or, more simply:

> Fools say in their hearts, 'There is no God.' (14: 1; 53: 1)

Scepticism about the power, reality, or justice of God is also heard occasionally in the prophetic books; as for example, when the people of Jerusalem are reported as saying, 'Yahweh will not do good, nor will he do ill' (Zeph. 1: 12; cf. Ezek. 8: 12; 9: 9). To this we must add that the prospect of wickedness unrequited or, worse, rewarded with temporal prosperity, could present an insuperable obstacle to the faith of those who remained faithful. So we hear, again in the psalms, laments that God has forgotten, that he has hidden his face, that perhaps he is not aware of what is going on (e.g. Pss. 10: 11; 73: 11; 125: 3). The sages also attest that the experience of adversity can lead a person to breaking point. As one proverb puts it:

> One's own folly leads to ruin,
> > yet the heart rages against Yahweh. (Prov. 19: 3)

At some time during the Persian period people were complaining that 'everyone who does evil is good in the sight of Yahweh', leading to the question, 'Where is the God of justice?' (Mal. 2: 17). Clearly, then, a conflict between the theory of moral causality and experience could easily raise questions about the ethical character of God as the sustainer of the moral order.

The shortest, and certainly the most obscure section of Proverbs, is attributed to a certain Agur ben-Yakeh (Prov. 30: 1–6). The textual obscurity of this short passage, reflected in the widely differing English versions, may well be the result of a deliberate attempt at some point in the editorial process to conceal sentiments too much at odds with orthodox beliefs. Any interpretation, therefore, will be hypothetical. A possible reconstruction of the sage's opening words would run as follows:

> There is no god, there is no god, and I am weary . . .
> Surely I am too stupid to be human,
> I do not have human understanding,
> I have not learned wisdom,
> > nor have I knowledge of the holy ones.

Whoever the author was (and some scholars think that the name is symbolic or a kind of cryptogram), he or she was struggling with the meaning of existence, including the possibility of a morally meaningful universe. There follows a series of rhetorical questions:

> Who has ascended to heaven and come down?
>> Who has gathered the wind in the hollow of the hand?
> Who has wrapped up the waters in a garment?
>> Who has established all the ends of the earth?
> What is the person's name?
>> And what is the name of the person's child?
>> Surely you know!

These are riddles and enigmas, especially the last two questions which probably bear on the obscure name of the putative author in the title. There is an ironic quality to the questioning, reminiscent of God's address to Job out of the whirlwind (Job 38). The questions seem to be addressed to the sceptic's 'learned colleagues' who seem to know everything about God and the world that is to be known. The approach is therefore not essentially different from that of Qoheleth, to be discussed shortly, though the latter affirms the reality of God while denying that we can know anything about his nature and operations. A final comment to the words of Agur (Prov. 30: 5–6) states that God has made himself known through his word and discourages the kind of theological speculation which, in the case of Agur, ended in frustration and negation.

This enigmatic text is one of the later components of Proverbs, perhaps from the late Persian or early Hellenistic period. About the same time the Chronicler was writing his version of the history from David to Ezra and Nehemiah (1 and 2 Chronicles, Ezra, Nehemiah). Like his principal source, the Deuteronomic History (Joshua, Judges, Samuel, Kings), the author sees the link between act and consequence as one of the keys for understanding the course of events and, at times, formulates it quite explicitly. In order to explain how Manasseh, a reprobate according to 2 Kings 21, could have ruled so long, he adds an account of how he repented and even has him carrying out religious reforms in the capital (2 Chr. 33: 10–17). Josiah, on the other hand, was a good king who nevertheless inexplicably died young. The Chronicler, therefore, adds a notice to the effect that he wilfully disregarded a divine oracle communicated through the Egyptian king (2 Chr. 35: 21–2). Taken together with the sayings of Agur and Qoheleth, this may serve to show that quite different points of view could be proposed during roughly the same period of time, and therefore will remind us that what is known as 'the religion of Israel' must be understood to take in quite different and even conflicting perspectives and opinions.

The Chronicler's determination to bring events into line with theological doctrine shows the urgency of the problem posed by the historical experience of Israel. During the disastrous period from the death of Josiah in 609 to the destruction of Jerusalem by the Babylonians in 587 or 586 BCE the problem for many became insoluble. Understandably, it has left a deep imprint on the writings which have survived from that time. One or two examples will have to suffice.

Written shortly after the tragic death of Josiah in 609, Habakkuk opens with an agonizing appeal for divine justice to be manifest:

> Yahweh, how long shall I cry for help,
>   and you will not hear?
> Or cry to thee, 'Violence!'
>   and you will not save?   (1: 2)

The note of agony is also heard in certain psalm-like passages in Jeremiah (e.g. 12: 1–4) and in hymns which, if they do not come from that time, reflect such a situation of total destitution (e.g. Pss. 44; 74; 79). A lament, possibly composed shortly after the fall of Jerusalem, poses the issue more sharply:

> Our ancestors sinned; they are no more;
>   and we bear their iniquities.   (Lam. 5: 7)

It also found expression in a proverb which circulated at that time: 'the ancestors have eaten sour grapes and the children's teeth are set on edge' (Jer. 31: 29–30; Ezek. 18: 2). The issue, then, was the fate of the innocent caught in the destructive flow of events which people had been taught to think were under the control of a powerful and just God. Given traditional religious beliefs, the massive disasters of the early sixth century BCE could only mean that either Yahweh was powerless to prevent them happening, or that he didn't care, or that he had decided to punish his people in a manner totally out of proportion to their wrongdoing. Hence the accusation of injustice levelled against God—'the way of Yahweh is not just' (Ezek. 18: 25, 29; 33: 17, 20).

One of those most concerned to counter this charge was Ezekiel, a prophet deported to Babylon shortly before the fall of Jerusalem. He argued that each generation, indeed each individual, stood on its own in the matter of moral responsibility and the imputation of guilt. Using the traditional form of casuistic or common law, he presented the test case of a family through three generations: a good man who has an evil son who, in his turn, has a son who does not follow his father's bad example. The conclusion: there is no carry-over from one generation to the next by virtue of the way divine justice is administered, and the point is reinforced by emphasizing the possibility of conversion (Ezek. 18: 5–29, cf. 33: 10–20). Elsewhere Ezekiel applied the same principle to the destruction of Jerusalem. In a vision dated five years before that event took place, he recorded that the righteous few were marked with a cross which guaranteed their survival (9: 1–11).

Since it was natural to conceive of divine justice as in some way analogous with judicial procedures in force in the society, Ezekiel's argument can be read simply as an acknowledgement that the justice of God must, at the least, come up to the best standards according to which human justice is administered. In the Deuteronomic law book the principle of corporate liability continued in force only in the exceptional cases of apostasy and homicide (Deut. 13: 12–18; 21: 1–9). In all other cases the emphasis is firmly on the responsibility of the individual:

Parents shall not be put to death for their children, nor shall children be put to death for their parents; only for their own crimes may persons be put to death. (24: 16)

This is quite different from the old cultic confession in which Yahweh is said to visit the iniquity of the fathers upon the children to the third and fourth generation (Exod. 34: 7; Num. 14: 18). However, an interesting case of development can be seen in the decalogue which takes up this same formula but adds to it the phrase 'of those who hate me' (Exod. 20: 5; Deut. 5: 9). Clearly, the purpose of this addition is to state that, if there is solidarity in guilt between the generations, it is because the children imitate the sins of their parents and not by virtue of the way God administers justice. Ezekiel expresses the same point of view, taking up and developing a more mature and reflective approach to the moral responsibility of the individual.

If political disaster, as generally understood at that time, focused attention on the way the guilty affected the fate of the innocent, it also forced people to reflect on the other side of the issue. In other words, given the existence of some righteous people in the doomed city (Jerusalem), a reasonable assumption and a possibility acknowledged by Ezekiel, the question arises whether they could not have influenced God to spare the city, even if it meant leaving the unrighteous majority unpunished. Ezekiel himself ruled out the possibility in one of his typical case histories—as a learned priest he was thoroughly familiar with legal procedures: Take, he says, a land devastated by war, pestilence, and other disasters. If there live in it such models of righteousness as Noah, Daniel, and Job, they would save no one, not even their sons and daughters, but only themselves (14: 12–23). It seems that at this point Ezekiel is dependent on Jeremiah's account of a famine during which it was revealed to him that God would not listen to the prayers of a sinful people, not even if Moses and Samuel, those masters of intercessory prayer, stood before him (Jer. 14: 1—15: 4). This seems to reflect the conviction, shared by many, that the destruction of the city was due in large measure to the failure of prophetic intercession (Jer. 7: 16; 11: 14; Ezek. 9: 8–10).

It will be obvious that Ezekiel's solution to the problem of divine justice is not entirely satisfactory, since it fails to cover situations in which the righteous, such as the three worthies in his example, perish together with the presumed reprobates. This issue, and the question whether the righteous can influence the fate of the guilty, are addressed in a quite different way in the dialogue between Abraham and God over the fate of Sodom (Gen. 18: 22–33). God had decided to destroy the city on account of its moral depravity, thus raising the same issue of discriminating between the good and the wicked. Abraham makes the point with great force: 'Far be it from you to do such a thing, to slay the innocent with the guilty. Far be it from you!

Shall not the judge of all the earth give right judgement?' But there is also the question whether a certain critical mass of righteous people can save the city. As Abraham's dramatic intercession gets the minimum required number down from fifty to ten, it emerges that such a critical mass does not exist. Yet ten would have sufficed, and so the possibility of the righteous influencing the fate of the unrighteous is here affirmed whereas in Ezekiel it is denied—another example of divergent solutions and points of view within the biblical canon. The possibility of a salvific role for the righteous will be very important in later religious developments in Judaism and Christianity. It has connections with the prophetic Servant of Second Isaiah who will 'make many to be accounted righteous' (Isa. 53: 11). Still later it will re-emerge in the belief, expounded in the Midrash, that at any time in history there are thirty-six hidden saints whose righteousness sustains the world—a theme underlying André Schwarz-Bart's famous novel, *The Last of the Just*.

A final note about this fascinating episode: its unique literary character, unlike anything else in Genesis, together with the fact that Jerusalem is sometimes referred to in prophetic diatribe as Sodom (e.g. Isa. 1: 9–10; 3: 9; Jer. 23: 14), suggests that we read it as a later addition to the Sodom narrative which has in mind the destruction of Jerusalem and the theological questions to which that momentous event gave rise. The central issue was the fate of the righteous in a world—or city—over which the God of Israel claimed jurisdiction. We must now see how this issue was dealt with in a much longer composition, though one in other respects quite similar, from the post-exilic period.

Job

The protagonist of this book is one of the three righteous men (Noah, Daniel, Job) living in a devastated land who will not be able to save anyone but themselves by their righteousness (Ezek. 14: 12–20). The narrative setting is the long ago of the ancestors living among the people of the east (1: 3, cf. Gen. 29: 1), when wealth was measured by numerous servants and livestock, and longevity was the rule. The place is the land of Uz (1: 1), also known to the ancestors

(Gen. 22: 21). Like Abraham, Job is righteous, a servant of God (1: 8, cf. Gen. 26: 24), one who intercedes for others (42: 8–9, cf. Gen. 20: 7), who is tested by God and survives with his faith intact.

Like the Job of Ezekiel 14: 12–20 the protagonist, though righteous, cannot save even his children, much less the many others affected by the successive disasters—hostile raids and meteorological disturbances—which afflicted the land of Uz. He is therefore left to try to make sense of what had happened and to struggle for faith in a God who, though judge of all the earth, appears to destroy the innocent along with the guilty (9: 22–4, cf. Gen. 18: 25). He is also like Abraham in daring, though but dust and ashes (42: 6, cf. Gen. 18: 27), to demand that God live up to the best standards according to which human justice is administered.

The work is a product of Israelite sagedom, or perhaps the composition of a foreign (Arab?) sage taken over by an individual or scribal school in Judah during the Persian period. Job himself is identified as a *hakam* (sage) and teacher (4: 3; 15: 2; 29: 21), as are his interlocutors, even though their sayings are 'proverbs of ashes' (13: 12). Following procedures familiar to their tradition, they look to the world of nature for lessons for human life (26: 5–14; 36: 24—37: 24), and even God speaks as a sage in pointing to the wonders of the natural world and its flora and fauna (chs. 38–41). The learned use of mythological topoi is in evidence throughout—the first man, rebellion in heaven, the defeat and binding of the forces of chaos, mythic monsters such as Leviathan, Abaddon, Tannin, Rahab. What counts as authoritative for all members of the team debating with Job is the teaching of former sages (15: 18) reinforced by their own experience and observation (4: 7–11). In these respects, then, Job reveals itself to be a learned product of scholastic wisdom at a mature stage of its development.

If we have correctly identified the time of composition, during the two centuries (6th to 4th BCE) of Iranian control of the province of Judah (Yehud), we can go further and locate the author or translator among the upper-class, lay intelligentsia of the province, educated in the tradition of public morality and piety discussed in the previous chapter. In this respect the contestants on both sides of the debate subscribe to the same social code. Job is the head of a large and prosperous household (19: 13–16), an employer of slaves and day-labourers (7: 2; 31: 13–15), a wealthy landowner (29: 1–25; 31: 25, 38–40), and prominent in public affairs (29: 7–25; 30: 28; 31: 21). Both he and his opponents in the debate evince a strong sense of public service and enlightened concern for the poor (29: 24; 30: 25; 31: 16–23). They are also unanimously opposed to members of the same social class who violate social norms, oppress the poor, corrupt the judicial process, and even commit murder with impunity (24: 13–17). We might suppose that educated members of this class were intellectually, but probably not emotionally, prepared to cope with personal and social disaster. But, then, who would be prepared to cope with disasters of the magnitude of those with which Job was afflicted?

Since some of the most difficult problems in the interpretation of the book arise out of its structure, it may be useful to lay this out at once:

Narrative prologue: alternating scenes on earth and in
    heaven (1–2).
Job's monologue (3).
Debate between Job and the 'friends': Eliphaz, Zophar,
    Bildad (4–27).
  First series (4–14),
  Second series (15–21),
  Third series (22–7).
Poem on inaccessible wisdom (28).
Job's oath of clearance and summons to God to appear (29–31).
Elihu's contribution (32–7).
God answers Job, who submits (38: 1—40: 5, 40: 6—42: 6).
Narrative epilogue: Job restored to good estate (42: 7–17).

The main feature is a narrative framework enclosing a debate between Job and four sages ending in a direct appeal by Job to God that he appear and state his case. After the divine response to this appeal, Job submits and the matter is ended. Certain indications of editorial activity which disturb the logical order should be noted. The third series in the debate (chs. 22–7) is confused, and the confusion may be explained in part on the assumption that Zophar's contribution has been transferred, accidentally or deliberately, to Job. The poem on wisdom (28), one of the most powerful in the

Hebrew Bible, was originally an independent composition and is here attributed, not entirely appropriately, to Job. (It will be discussed at greater length in the last chapter of this book.) The lengthy harangue of the bombastic Elihu is clearly intrusive and quite unexpected after the notice that the words of Job are ended (31: 40). That it was added after the work was essentially complete is suggested by the allusions in it to God's answer to Job, quite apart from the fact that only three respondents had been introduced and are to reappear in the epilogue. The fact that Elihu is the only Israelite name among Job's interlocutors—the others are Arabic—suggests that this insertion was intended as an 'orthodox' critique of all parties in the debate up to that point. It delays the sequel to Job's summons, which is of course the appearance and reply of God. It seems, finally, that the book has preserved two accounts of God's answer and Job's reaction to his appearance.

A further point: it has long been noted that the narrative framework does not make a good fit with the body of the work. At the most obvious level, the long-suffering Job of the prologue undergoes a startling transformation once he begins to soliloquize and reply to his 'friends'. So also the latter, who keep silent and sympathetic vigil at the outset, progressively reveal themselves to be far from friendly as the debate gathers momentum. The God of the narrative prologue and epilogue is Yahweh, Israel's own God, whereas the God who is spoken of and who speaks in the body of the work bears the more generic names, common to Semitic antiquity, of El, Eloah, and Shaddai. More importantly, the narrative appears to affirm what it is the purpose of the debate to call into question, i.e., that innocence is always vindicated and guilt always punished. In the course of the debate Job is taken to task by God for his intemperate speech, while in the prose epilogue the 'friends' are castigated for not having spoken well of God. There is also the curious fact that the Satan, who appears at the beginning as the occasion of Job's atrocious suffering, is not heard of again.

There is also the fact that the epilogue does not work too well as the proverbial happy ending. Job ends up with several times as much livestock as before, in addition to which his relatives have a collection for him and get together to cheer him up. He also gets a new family, but we cannot forget, nor can he, that those who died as a result of the experiment stayed dead.

It is for these reasons that many commentators have been led to the conclusion that the debate, the purpose of which is to provide a new solution to the problem of undeserved suffering and the divine governance of the world, has been spliced into an old folktale which, in effect, reaffirms the traditional teaching of the sages on these issues. One problem with this view is, of course, the assumption that the final editor did not notice the discrepancy between the debate and its framework which is so obvious to the modern reader. One would have thought that this point could have been made more clearly by simply telling the story of a just man who, like Abraham, is tested by God, comes through with flying colours, and is eventually restored to good fortune. What calls for an explanation is precisely the juxtaposition of narrative and debate or, in other words, the final shape of the work irrespective of whatever editorial stages led up to it. And since, in its final form, it begins and ends in narrative it must be interpreted as a narrative work, which means that we must ask it what happens to the protagonist—and to others—in the course of it.

Beginning with the prologue which, with the epilogue, is in prose, Job is presented as a righteous man blessed with a large family and many possessions. His children were in the habit of celebrating the festivals in each other's houses, on which occasions Job would offer sacrifices to make amends for any secret sins which they might commit. Meanwhile, a different kind of assembly was taking place in heaven. The scenario here has clear analogies with other heavenly scenes in the Hebrew Bible, including the prophetic visions of Isaiah (6: 1–13) and Micaiah (1 Kgs. 22: 19–23). This last is worth a closer look. Summoned by king Ahab to give a favourable oracle before battle, Micaiah reported a vision in which Yahweh asked for a volunteer among the attendants at his court to go and deceive the king so that he should die in battle. One of these, referred to simply as the Spirit, offered to discharge the task by being a lying spirit in the mouth of the prophets. Yahweh consented: 'You are to entice him, and you shall succeed; go, do it.' The post-exilic prophet Zechariah also reported a vision in which Joshua the high priest was indicted unsuccessfully by the Satan standing at his right hand (Zech. 3: 1–5). This scenario of the divine court seems to have been borrowed from Canaanite mythology in which El, supreme God of the pantheon, is surrounded by lesser deities. The Satan, who is not, of course, the familiar figure of Christian imagination and art, appears as one of the attendants of the divine court in the act of making his report. As the name ('adversary' in Hebrew) suggests, his function is that of checking and testing the loyalty of Yahweh's subjects. This role is reminiscent of that of a Persian official known as 'the king's eye' or 'the king's ear' whose task was to tour a province or satrapy checking up on local officials, at times by acting as an *agent provocateur*.

So, on the subject of Job, the Satan suggests that his piety is interested; in effect, a function of his prosperity. This leads to a kind of wager or, worse, a laboratory experiment, in which the Satan is permitted to deprive him of everything to see if he will curse God and, by so doing, sever relations with him. The string of disasters which follows, which affects others in the land of Uz besides Job, is represented as directly flowing from this conversation in heaven to which the reader, but not Job, is privy. Yet Job does not sin by cursing God, not even at the suggestion of his wife, and not even when afflicted with a particularly atrocious form of skin disease.

The purpose of this prologue is not just to tell a story but to pose a problem. The suffering of the innocent is indeed attributable to God, being permitted as a test of integrity. The alternatives for the one subjected to this test are to accept it without question or to curse God, and to curse God means to attribute evil intent to him, to charge him with wrongdoing (1: 22). It is also important to note that the curse was a means of dissociating oneself from the party cursed. The manner of the testing raises, and is intended to raise, serious questions about the ethical character of God, questions which it is the purpose of the debate to explore. In this sense, at least, the prologue and the debate clearly belong together.

The opening soliloquy introduces a rather different Job who curses the night of his conception and the day of his birth, and voices his despair in dark images of stillbirth and death. To judge by their names, the debaters are Arab sages testifying, together with the Arabs Agur and Lemuel of Proverbs, to the reputation for wisdom enjoyed by the Edomites and Arabs. They are not intended to be straw men, mechanically reproducing arguments for Job to refute. On the contrary, they represent the best thinking available in the schools on the issue under discussion and their arguments are presented as serious options. Eliphaz opens the debate courteously, advancing the orthodox argument that innocence is always rewarded sooner or later, and adding the further lesson, for which the authority of a personal revelation is adduced, that no mortal is pure or wise enough to question God's dealings (4: 12–21). On this basis he tactfully suggests that Job examine his conscience, since only by confessing sin can some rationale of suffering and evil be maintained.

The second speaker, Bildad, proceeds on a somewhat more acrimonious note, explaining the death of Job's children on the grounds that God had allowed their (presumably secret) sins to catch up with them (8: 4). As for Job himself, he should consult the accumulated wisdom of the past which testifies that innocence is always vindicated, and that therefore his sufferings will come to an end if he is really as blameless as he claims to be. The third, Zophar, is the least accommodating of the three, accusing Job of wilful ignorance and stupidity in not acknowledging the infinite distance between God and humanity. He therefore also urges him to confess as a means of bringing his suffering to an end.

In his replies, Job expresses his hatred of life and longing for death, not because of his sufferings in themselves, but because God has, inexplicably, become his enemy. And here it is important to note that he desires death not because he hopes that injustice will be righted in a life after death, but only to put an end to the consciousness of pain (significantly, he never contemplates suicide). Life after death is, in fact, subsequently ruled out (see 7: 9–10). It is ironic that the only passage in the book likely to be familiar to the general reader—owing to the popularity of Handel's *Messiah*—is widely interpreted as an affirmation of the hope for immortality or resurrection:

> For I know that my redeemer lives,
>   and that at the last he will stand upon the earth;
> and after my skin has been thus destroyed,
>   then in my flesh I shall see God. (19: 25–6)

As it stands, the meaning is far from clear, and the reason is that the passage is textually corrupt, almost beyond recovery, a fate which often befalls controversial texts. The context suggests that Job is here expressing the desire that his case be recorded indelibly in writing in the hope of an at least posthumous vindication when the decisive witness of his innocence, to whom he despairingly appeals throughout the book (9: 32–3; 16: 19–21; 33: 23–4), will take his stand in court. In any case, as we have just seen, the finality of death is clearly affirmed by Job at other points in the debate (see also 10: 20–2; 14: 7–12), and it is a sound exegetical principle to interpret obscure passages in the light of those which are less obscure.

The literary ability which is one of the characteristics of Israel's sages is abundantly in evidence in this first series of arguments and counter-arguments. So, for example, the author makes use of familiar hymn forms, putting psalms of individual lamentation into Job's mouth (e.g. 7: 1–11) while his opponents quote psalms of trust and confidence at him (e.g. 5: 17–27). Proverbs are also traded back and forth—not surprisingly, since it is a contest of sages—and there are other literary devices in use in the schools such as the rhetorical question (e.g. 6: 5–6). But most noteworthy is the use of forensic terminology, the language of the courtroom, especially in Job's answer to Bildad (9–10). He speaks of the impossibility of a fair trial when God is both accuser and judge, of issuing, or responding to, a summons to appear in court, of arguing his case with the assistance of a counsel for the defence, and so on. It seems that the author has chosen this forensic model deliberately as a means of presenting the case for both parties, God and Job. At the beginning Job is in the dock; later it is God's turn. And since the same kind of legal language is used elsewhere in the Hebrew Bible in speaking of the covenant between God and the people (e.g. in the prophetic indictment of Israel for covenant infidelity), the likelihood is increased that the book is concerned with the crisis not just of an individual but of the nation. We have seen how the disasters of the early sixth century BCE gave rise to the gravest theological problems and called into question the justice of God and his fidelity to the covenant made with the ancestors.

Eliphaz opens the second round of the debate by raising the question of authority, a matter of great importance for the sages. One could appeal to ancient tradition or, with the prophets, to personal revelation. In neither respect did Job qualify, since he was not the first man nor had he been admitted to the secret conclave of God (15: 7–8). Indeed, he was not even all that old that he should speak

with such assurance (15: 10). By now, however, it is apparent that
Job is no longer interested in refuting arguments of his interlocutors;
it is a matter between himself and God alone. And so he takes his
life in his hands in accusing God of indifference to the human condition, of massively undermining human hope, even of murder;

> It is all one; therefore I say,
>   he destroys both the blameless and the wicked.
> When disaster brings sudden death,
>   he mocks at the calamity of the innocent.
> The earth is given into the hands of the wicked;
>   he covers the faces of its judges—
>   if it is not he, who then is it? (9: 22–4)

> The waters wear away the stones . . .
>   so you destroy the hope of mortals. (14: 19)

> O earth, cover not my blood,
>   and let my cry find no resting place! (16: 18)

In the third and last series the contrasting positions are stated in
their most extreme and stark form, so much so that the disjointed
sequence of speakers and ideas is probably due to later attempts to
mitigate the violence of the accusations levelled against the God of
traditional religion. As it is, Job conjures up a terrible vision of a
world where moral chaos rules supreme, in which power is triumphant and the poor trampled into the ground, over which presides a God who chooses not to intervene. His accusation may be
translated as follows:

> From the city the dying groan,
>   the throat of the wounded cries,
>   yet God sees nothing amiss. (24: 12)

In a different context all of this would be nothing more nor less than
blasphemy; but with Job it arises, paradoxically, from his refusal to
break off relations with God, to take his wife's advice to 'curse God
and die'. Since he speaks in the assurance that 'a godless man shall
not come before him' (13: 16), it is, in effect, a violent form of prayer
uttered *in extremis*.

The poem on wisdom (ch. 28), which will be discussed at length
in Chapter 6, is ascribed to Job in the present state of the text (27:

1). Since, however, the passage immediately preceding (27: 13–23) is a fairly conventional description of how the wicked man comes to a bad end, the order has certainly been disturbed. It would, in addition, be rather surprising to find Job at this point equating wisdom with the 'fear of Yahweh' (28: 28). Job's final discourse (29–31) contrasts an earlier time, when God was his friend, with present miseries in the manner of those psalms of lamentation which open with a recital of past divine favours, go on to describe present misfortunes, and end with an appeal to God to remember and make his presence felt (e.g. Ps. 89). The climax of his peroration, and of the debate as a whole, is the oath of clearance couched in the form of confession of innocence—not unlike the Egyptian Books of the Dead which contain a catalogue of evil deeds not done—and sealed with self-imposed curses. At this point the forensic metaphor is quite explicit. The situation is as follows. In Israelite legal practice the taking of the oath of clearance by an accused party, even in capital cases, resulted in the accusation being dropped and the accused left to his own devices. The sages therefore are at last silenced and Job summons God to appear and state his case—in effect, issues a subpoena (31: 35–7). God does appear, but not until Elihu, the angry young man of the book, has had his say, and a lengthy say at that.

Since the contribution of Elihu comes from a later hand, we may suppose that it was added out of dissatisfaction with the debate, or at least because it was thought something essential had been omitted. It is even possible that these speeches were added to a book which ended with the colophon, 'the words of Job are ended' (31: 40), and that therefore they were not meant to be a final judgement on the debate. And in fact Elihu does find both parties deficient in that God, by his nature, is immeasurably superior to both the rationalizations of the sages and the importunate demands of Job. He also stresses the absolute freedom of God who cannot be questioned and who makes himself known on his own terms and in his own ways (e.g. 33: 12–18; 35: 6–7). Suffering is a divine discipline, and the appropriate response is an attitude of humble acceptance (33: 19–28). These are not unimportant considerations, even though expressed without grace or consideration for the audience, and highlight once again the variety and the depth of reflection on theological issues among the scribes of the Second Temple period.

God finally answers Job's summons, but not in the way Job intended or anticipated. The voice from the whirlwind is patterned on prophetic descriptions of the theophany:

> You will be visited by Yahweh of hosts
> with thunder and earthquake and great noise,
> with whirlwind and tempest, and the flame of a devouring
> fire. (Isa. 29: 6)

The actual message, however, reflects the sages' learned preoccupations with the wonders of nature; witness the detailed descriptions of ostrich (39: 13–18), horse (39: 19–25), hawk (39: 26–30), hippopotamus (40: 15–24), and crocodile (41: 1–34). But the important point is that the God who reveals himself to Job is not a God who can be circumscribed by learned debate in the schools, or about whom calculations can be made, or with whom contractual arrangements can be drawn up. In this respect the author reflects the shift towards a more transcendental and universalist understanding of Yahweh to which the national disasters of the sixth century certainly contributed. In that sense, both Job and his learned colleagues stand under judgement.

For many readers, however, there will still be the scandal that God does not address himself to Job's question or, what is even worse, answers the question of justice with a display of power which simply confirms the existence of the problem. This may mean that there is simply no answer to the problem so posed, or that faith must not be contingent upon receiving a divine assurance that it will all turn out well in the end. And, when all is said and done, God does finally show at least that he is present. In this respect, comparison with Psalm 73, a didactic rather than cultic composition, may be useful. The poet begins with the same problem as Job, that of the triumph of evil in a world believed to be under the governance of a just God. There is no theoretical solution, but none is needed once the perplexed questioner enters the sanctuary, experiences the reality of the divine presence and, like Job, makes his confession:

> When my soul was embittered,
> when I was pricked in heart,
> I was stupid and ignorant,
> I was like a brute beast toward you.

> Nevertheless I am continually with you;
>> you hold my right hand . . .   (Ps. 73: 21–30)

> I had heard of you by the hearing of the ear,
>> but now my eye sees you;
> therefore I despise myself,
>> and repent in dust and ashes.   (Job 42: 5–6)

To come back, finally, to the narrative character of the work: something happens to Job, something within his own painful experience which changes everything. The book might well have ended here, with his confession and submission (42: 6). Indeed, the fragmentary targum or paraphrase of Job from the eleventh cave at Qumran (11QtgJob), which ends at 42: 11, shows that there was some hesitation as to where the book should end as late as the second century BCE when the targum was written. The epilogue, at any rate, does no more than suggest that, if the traditional teaching on retribution continues in force, it must be in a form which allows faith to be independent of self-interest and which takes account of the intractable and painful data of experience.

Qoheleth

The problem with which the author of Job struggled was obviously not confined to one place or time, however critical. A Sumerian scribal composition from the first half of the second millennium BCE, translated under the title of 'The Sumerian Job' or 'A Man and His God', speaks of an innocent young man who, like Job, is afflicted with sickness. Calumniated on this account by his associates, who attribute his condition to a god's anger brought about by sin, he prays earnestly and confesses his sins with the result that his affliction is turned into joy. Unlike Job, however, he does not question divine justice. We come upon a similar situation in a Babylonian psalm entitled 'I will praise the lord of wisdom' (*ludlul bel nemeqi*). As a result of sickness, the worshipper has been slandered and ostracized. He nevertheless continues in his devotion to the Babylonian god Marduk whose ways are acknowledged to be inscrutable, and eventually receives assurance in a dream of a happy outcome.

A more speculative and didactic composition from a somewhat later time, translated under the title 'The Babylonian Theodicy', presents a dialogue between an innocent sufferer and a friendly sage. Like Job, the former contrasts his misfortune with the prosperity of the wicked, is accused of impiety for his pains, and is assured that the wicked will get their deserts sooner or later. The proper response to suffering is piety towards the gods, even while admitting that the world created by them is flawed.

Strictly speaking, this last is the only composition from the ancient Near East which deals with the problem of divine justice and is therefore comparable to the biblical Job. There are writings which describe a reversal of fortune brought about by divine intervention in the manner of the Job epilogue. The Keret (Kirtu?) epic from Bronze Age Ugarit, for example, tells of a king who lost his entire family and eventually gained another with the help of the gods. What is lacking, however, is the essential element of focusing on the action and character of the deity as problematic.

Quite different is the so-called 'Dialogue of Pessimism', an extraordinary Mesopotamian text from the first millennium BCE, where the starting point is not suffering and deprivation but ennui. A lord makes a series of proposals to do certain things such as dining, going for a ride in the country, and so on, and his servant urges him to do so, providing what appear to be excellent reasons; whereupon the lord changes his mind and the servant comes up with even stronger reasons for not doing them. The conversation goes somewhat as follows:

'Servant, listen to me.' 'Yes, master, yes.' 'I am going to make love to a woman.' 'So make love, master, make love. The man who makes love to a woman forgets sorrow and worry.' 'No, servant, I will not make love to a woman.' 'Do not make love, master, do not make love. A woman is a pitfall, a hole, a ditch, a woman is a sharp iron dagger that slits a man's throat.'

Depressingly familiar, these sentiments, not unlike Qoheleth's 'I found more bitter than death the woman who is a trap, whose heart is snares and nets, whose hands are fetters' (7: 26). Not without a certain cynical humour, the dialogue makes short shrift of the 'consolations of religion' and proceeds to its terminus in the decision of

the lord to commit suicide and take the servant with him. Compari-
sons are often made between this text and the biblical Ecclesiastes
(Qoheleth) but, as we shall now see, the similarity is more apparent
than real.

Qoheleth occurs as a personal name in the title of the book (1: 1),
but in the postscript (12: 8) and the body of the work (7: 27) it carries the article and therefore stands for an office or function. The
Old Greek translation (Septuagint) and the Vulgate, followed by
RSV, interpret this as an ecclesiastical office (*ecclesiastes*, preacher),
but even a rapid glance at the book reveals that there is little ecclesiastical about its author. The Hebrew term should therefore be ren-
dered 'teacher' or perhaps 'orator'. The attribution to Solomon,
made in the title but sustained only in the first part of the work (1:
12—2: 26), is of course a literary fiction. Its significance is that it
places the work within the established sapiential tradition deriving
from Solomon. It also allowed the author to direct a radical criticism
at the optimism, pragmatism, and self-assurance of that tradition
from within.

Taking on the mantle of the wisest of kings also, in all probability, suggested the form of the work, which is that of a royal testament featuring personal reminiscence. A familiar type of instruction
in ancient Egypt, it would have seemed appropriate during the epoch
of Ptolemaic rule—the third century BCE—when the book was probably written. For the Ptolemies, who controlled a large empire,
including Palestine, from Alexandria in Egypt, saw themselves as
successors of the pharaohs and promoted a revival of pharaonic style
both in life and letters.

Whatever the original form of the work, a later scribe and editor
assigned it to the more familiar category of 'sayings of the sages' (12:
9–11, cf. Prov. 1: 6; 22: 17, 23). The author belonged to the ranks
of the professional sages and teachers; the title suggests, in fact, that
he came to be known as *the* teacher, though editorial comments
added at the end of the book suggest that not all approved of his
work. These comments, from at least two different hands, may be
translated as follows:

Not content with attaining wisdom himself [or: in addition to being a
sage], Qoheleth gave instruction to the public.

Qoheleth weighed, examined, and edited many aphorisms, seeking to identify appropriate sayings and recording truthful sayings plainly.

The sayings of the sages are like goads, and like nails firmly fixed are the collections of sayings . . . [unintelligible].

My son, beware of anything beyond these; of making many books there is no end, and much study is a weariness of the flesh.

The end of the matter: all has been heard. Fear God and keep his commandments, for this is the sum total of everyone's duty. For God will bring every deed into judgement, including every hidden thing, whether good or evil.

This editorial postscript begins with an *apologia* for the author's work which must have been controversial. It identifies him as a sage and teacher who worked with proverbs, as the book in fact demonstrates, and found the right language to make his students think for themselves. The last two comments are much less positive. Their drift seems to be that this sort of speculative approach to life is all right, but the best advice is to keep it simple. If the last comment— fear God and keep his commandments in the light of divine judgement—is intended as a summary of the book, it may presuppose the insertion into it at various points of more orthodox sentiments (e.g. 3: 17; 7: 18; 8: 12–13; 11: 9) which would then help to explain why Ecclesiastes won acceptance into the scriptural canon. Whether the author himself would have agreed with it as an adequate summary of his own thinking is another matter.

The first thing to note is that Qoheleth writes within the tradition of the sages; hence his insistence on observation, experience, investigation, and enquiry—'I applied my mind to seek and search out by wisdom all that is done under heaven' (1: 13). As one of his editors notes, he works with traditional proverbial material, but he does so in his own way. He cites, for example, a proverb embodying the typical contrast between the wise person and the fool:

> The wise have eyes in their head,
> but fools walk in darkness,

and then adds the comment that it doesn't make any difference since both wise and fools are subject to the same fate (2: 14). At other times he will simply juxtapose two proverbs which cancel each other out—as, for example:

> Fools fold their hands,
>   and consume their own flesh

followed immediately by

> Better is a handful with quiet
>   than two handfuls with toil.   (4: 5–6)

We shall see other instances in which he cites or comments on traditional verities in a way which he must have known would be offensive to pious ears. In general, the new, the modern element in Qoheleth is the personal and autobiographical tone—I applied my mind, I saw, I said to myself, this is what I have found, adding one thing to another to see what it all amounts to.

Though Ecclesiastes has generally been thought to lack any firm structure, the first part at least (1: 3—2: 26) presents a consistent and well-arranged argument. After the tone is set with a refrain which sounds like a tolling bell throughout the work—'emptiness, emptiness, all is empty' (NEB)—Qoheleth argues that both human history and the phenomena of nature suggest an endless, predetermined cyclical process which excludes novelty and deprives human effort of ultimate significance. This conclusion is confirmed by personal experience; and here the author speaks in the person of Solomon. The search for pleasure and wisdom, the amassing of wealth, the doing of great deeds—all of these end in frustration since they end in death and, in due time, oblivion. The first and natural reaction is despair—hatred of life and self-hatred—which, however, unlike the Mesopotamian text referred to a moment ago, does not end in suicide. On the contrary, Qoheleth leads us from the certainty of death to the positive acceptance of life and whatever limited satisfactions it has to offer:

There is nothing better for mortals than to eat and drink, and find enjoyment in their toil. This also, I saw, is from the hand of God.   (2: 24)

We find here, right at the beginning, a cardinal point in the teaching of this exceptional thinker. Death undermines the structures of meaning by which the wisdom tradition makes sense of life. It also frustrates the practical means by which it seeks to bring human action under the control of rationality. More than any other event, it lies outside human control and defies explanation. For Qoheleth, it is, quite simply *fate* (2: 14–15; 3: 19; 9: 2–3), an idea found nowhere else in the Hebrew Bible and, in fact, foreign to biblical thought. (Isa. 65: 11 refers to Gad and Meni, gods of fortune, but their cult is condemned.) Yet, paradoxically, wherever this conclusion is reached, it is followed at once by the affirmation of life, with all its limitations, as the *portion* of humankind under the inscrutable dispensation of God (3: 22; 5: 18; 9: 9). The practical and ethical corollary is that only when death is accepted without the illusions which the fear of death so easily generates can one really begin to accept life as a gift and *live*.

It is therefore extremely important to distinguish Qoheleth's point of view from the kind of despairing hedonism which the thought of the finality of death often inspires. The contrast will be apparent in the words which the author of the Wisdom of Solomon (to be discussed in Ch. 6) puts in the mouth of the Jew who has abandoned his traditional religion under the allure of popular Epicurean philosophy:

> Short and sorrowful is our life,
> and there is no remedy when a life comes to its end,
> and no one has been known to return from Hades.
> For we were born by mere chance,
> and hereafter we shall be as though we had never
> been . . .
> For our allotted time is the passing of a shadow,
> and there is no return from our death,
> because it is sealed up and no one turns back.
> Come, therefore, let us enjoy the good things that
> exist,
> and make use of the creation to the full, as in youth.
> Let us take our fill of costly wine and perfumes,
> and let no flower of spring pass us by.
> Let us crown ourselves with rosebuds before they
> wither.
> Let none of us fail to share in our revelry,

> everywhere let us leave signs of enjoyment,
> because this is our portion, and this is our lot.
>
> (Wisd. 2: 1–9)

While it is entirely possible that Qoheleth was familiar with Epicurean philosophy—of which, incidentally, this quotation is something of a caricature—his philosophy of death does not derive from this source. If there is any analogy with philosophical views of Late Antiquity, it would be with the Stoic distinction between the things which are and are not within our control, as expounded, for example, in the *Moral Discourses* of Epictetus. Of all things death is least under our control, and to accept this situation is to free the mind from a major source of crippling anxiety. But whatever possible analogies may be proposed, it seems that Qoheleth is offering a positive answer to the numbing question which death poses to any reflective person.

Qoheleth also has his own answer to the most fundamental problem discussed in the schools, that of the divine governance of the world. He notes that where one would expect, following the traditional line, to find justice triumphant in the world, what one finds is the opposite (3: 16–4: 3). At this point, typically, he cites the standard answer, only now it includes the possibility of a post-mortem settling of accounts:

I said in my heart, God will judge the righteous and the wicked, for he has appointed a time for every matter, and for every work. (3: 17)

but then he goes on to ask: how do we know that this world is not all that there is? how can we find comfort in these contemporary speculations about survival of death and astral immortality?

I said in my heart with regard to human beings that God is testing them to show that they are but animals. For the fate of humans and the fate of animals is the same; as one dies, so dies the other. They all have the same breath, and humans have no advantage over the animals; for all is vanity. All go to one place; all are from the dust, and all turn to dust again. Who knows whether the human spirit goes upward and the spirit of animals goes downward to the earth? (3: 18–21)

The didactic poem to which Qoheleth refers in speaking of a time appointed by God, together with its commentary (3: 1–15), follows the first section about the circle of time and seasons (chs. 1–2) and develops further the author's philosophical view of time in relation to the divine dispensation. Since there is nothing in the poem itself (3: 2–8) characteristic of Qoheleth, it may be an independent composition, and therefore the longest of the citations in the book on which the author comments. The poem reflects the traditional teaching that there is an appropriate time for each human act—an important consideration since it is part of wisdom to do everything at the proper time. In his brief commentary (vv. 9–15) Qoheleth agrees with the traditional view on the importance of the *timing* of our actions—e.g. when to speak and keep quiet (Prov. 15: 23)—but adds that the ability to apply this principle is contingent on knowing the dispositions of God with respect to human existence. Each of our moments is measured on the continuum of God's time (translated 'eternity' in RSV and 'a sense of past and future' in NRSV); the human mind can arrive at the point of acknowledging that this is so, but this knowledge does not translate into the ability to act appropriately, to exercise control over one's life. God has predetermined everything; nothing can be changed; the circle is closed (3: 14–15). Time is God's time, but we do not have the key to crack the code. This is a major theme of Qoheleth which recurs throughout the work. Thus, in keeping with his method of subjecting traditional gnomic wisdom to criticism, he quotes a proverb:

> What is crooked cannot be made straight,
> and what is lacking cannot be counted.   (1: 15)

and restates it, at a later point, with astonishing theological candour:

> Consider the work of God;
> who can make straight what he has made crooked?   (7: 13)

This work of God, he goes on to say, is the fortuitous incidence of good and evil fortune to which experience attests; and it happens so that we may never know what the future holds (3: 14, cf. 8: 6–7). The sages claim to be able to fathom what goes on on earth, to make sense of it as God's work, but they are mistaken (8: 17). If the sages were right, things would work out as they predict, but it does not happen that way. Humankind is the creature of chance, at the mercy of circumstances beyond its control (9: 11–12).

The inescapable consequence of this position is that the link between act and consequence, and therefore the idea of divine retribution, is called into question. This leads quite logically to the issue of unrequited evil and injustice which Qoheleth goes on to address (3: 16—4: 3). As always, he begins with experience: 'Moreover I saw under the sun that in the place of justice, wickedness was there, and in the place of righteousness, wickedness was there as well' (3: 16). He then, typically, quotes an orthodox proverb to the effect that in due time the scandal of triumphant injustice will be righted by God (3: 17), refutes it in the name of actual experience, and queries current speculations about post-mortem beatitude. His advice is to put aside such speculation and get on with the job of living.

Unlike the prophets, Qoheleth does not propose to do anything about injustice in the world. It is one of those things outside our control that we must learn to live with—an attitude probably shared by many whose lives were controlled by the massive bureaucratic machine of the Ptolemaic monarchy (cf. 5: 8–20; 8: 2–9). He does, however, offer some penetrating reflections on the contemporary rat race (4: 4–16). With the help of proverbs (vv. 5, 6, 9–13) he notes how rivalry, competition, keeping up with others, lead to isolation and alienation. People never stop to ask, 'Why am I doing all this?' His conclusion: that human companionship, genuine society, is the only antidote to the inevitable miseries and vexations of life.

There can be no doubt that for Qoheleth the fundamental issue is religious; that is to say, it has to do with what we can know about God and what consequences follow from that knowledge. His relationship to the traditional and ancestral religion is tenuous to say the least, he refers always to 'the deity' never to Yahweh, and his attitude to the external expressions of that religion—animal sacrifice, prayer, vows, etc.—is critical and detached. His God is not one who suffers fools gladly:

Guard your steps when you go to the house of God; to draw near to listen is better than the sacrifice offered by fools; for they do not know how to keep from doing evil. Never be rash with your mouth, nor let your heart be quick to utter a word before God, for God is in heaven, and you upon earth; therefore let your words be few . . . when you make a vow to God, do not delay fulfilling it; for he has no pleasure in fools. Fulfil what you vow. It is better that you should not vow than that you should vow and not fulfil it.   (5: 1–5)

God is transcendent and unknowable. Everything is under his control, but whether in love or hate we do not know (9: 1); nor does he vouchsafe to satisfy the human demand for justice. Yet the practical outcome is not denial or rejection of God but an attitude of fear and reverence (3: 14; 5: 7; 7: 18), together with a positive ethic of grateful acceptance of life as a fragile gift. We are reminded again of Epictetus, the Stoic philosopher who wrote some three centuries later:

Whenever you grow attached to something, do not act as though it were one of those things that cannot be taken away, but as though it were something like a jar or a crystal goblet, so that when it breaks you will remember what it was like, and not be troubled. So too in life; if you kiss your child, your brother, your friend, never allow your fancy free rein . . . remind yourself that the object of your love is mortal . . . it has been given you for the present, not inseparably, nor for ever, but like a fig, or a cluster of grapes, at a fixed season of the year, and that if you hanker for it in the winter you are a fool. (*Moral Discourses*, ch. 24)

Since we are almost completely in the dark with regard to Jewish intellectual life in the third century BCE we can only speculate about the social and cultural milieu in which the author moved. There were no doubt many of the educated upper classes who, like Qoheleth, were intellectually serious but rather detached from traditional religious ideas and practices. It was also in such milieux that new philosophical ideas were beginning to circulate, conspicuously those of the early Stoics, Zeno, Cleanthes, and Chrysippus. While these Stoics dealt with the big philosophical issues—fate, free will, time, and so on—the basic issue for them, as for Qoheleth, was ethical—what is good for human beings to do under heaven for the brief span of their lives (Eccles.2: 3). Qoheleth, it seems, was familiar with Stoic ideas about time and fate but on these issues, as on others, he went his own way.

It appears, at any rate, that by that time, the middle or later decades of the third century BCE, the traditional wisdom of the schools was facing formidable challenges from other systems and ways of viewing reality. New ways of thinking, new perspectives on reality, however, generally go in tandem with social and political changes. We should therefore note Qoheleth's addiction to economic terminology and metaphor. He is obsessed with toil as the defining characteristic of human activity, refers often to trade and business ventures that go awry, to making a profit, accumulating wealth, and the like. He knows all about economic exploitation but doesn't think anything can be done about it; it is simply a by-product of the working of the vast bureaucratic machinery of the Ptolemaic empire.

A batch of papyri discovered in Egypt in 1915 affords us a rare glimpse into the workings of that bureaucracy in Qoheleth's day. They are part of the archive of a certain Zeno, a highly placed estate agent with business interests in Palestine. They testify to an enormous gap between rich and poor and a crippling burden of taxes collected by rapacious tax farmers. Josephus (*Antiquities*, 12: 154–236) fills out the picture with his account of Joseph of the Jewish Tobiad family, also mentioned in the papyri, who won the bidding for tax collecting in Syria and Palestine, made a huge fortune, and passed it on to his son Hyrcanus. The latter fell out of favour with the Seleucid king Antiochus IV, retired to his estate in Transjordan and committed suicide.

The Zeno papyri and Josephus open a small window on a Jewish world very different from the world of priests, prophets, and sages, but a world with which we imagine Qoheleth to have been familiar. This is not to say that he would have endorsed the amorality of the Tobiads, for he has his own hard-won convictions, a kind of stripped-down Judaism and Jewish ethic based on a realistic assessment of human limitations and the acceptance of death.

It is of the greatest interest that those responsible for the final selection of texts in the Hebrew Bible have left in this critique of wisdom, including theological wisdom, from the inside; and it certainly did not happen by oversight. Qoheleth rejects the claim of his colleagues to give a rational account of the world and of the 'work of God' as it impinges on it (8: 16–17); and he does so after a lifetime engaged in the same arduous endeavour:

All this I have tested by wisdom; I said, 'I will be wise'; but it was far from me. That which is, is far off, and deep, very deep; who can find it out?   (7: 23–4)

The problem remains

The title Ecclesiasticus derives from the Latin and means 'church book'. The reason for the title, apparently, is that this composition, though not accepted into the Christian canon, was deemed eminently suitable for liturgical use. Its author was a certain Jesus ben Sira, a Jerusalemite scribe and teacher who wrote in Hebrew in the early decades of the second century BCE. He seems to have been familiar with Qoheleth's work and even echoes his sentiments here and there (e.g. Ecclus. 7: 36; 11: 18–19; 18: 22–3). But while he too discourses on human misery (e.g. 40: 1–11) he has little of the intellectual boldness and originality of his predecessor. In fact, he warns against the dangers of speculative thought:

> Neither seek what is too difficult for you,
>   nor investigate what is beyond your power.
> Reflect upon what you have been commanded,
>   for what is hidden is not your concern.
> Do not meddle in matters that are beyond you,
>   for more than you can understand has been shown you.
> For their conceit has led many astray,
>   and wrong opinion has impaired their judgement.
>
>   (3: 21–4)

In these and similar statements he may even have had Qoheleth in mind. A polemical note is also detectable in his strong affirmation of free will and denial that God is in any way responsible for moral incapacity and its toll in human suffering (15: 11–20). Sin is of human not divine origin, deriving as it does from the evil impulse rooted in human nature which, however, can be resisted through prayer and religious observance. Apart from tracing this proclivity to evil back to the first couple (25: 24), a theological position which will be further developed in Jewish and early Christian writings (e.g. Wisd. 2: 23–4; Rom. 5: 12), Ben Sira does not speculate on it over-much or treat it as problematic. He is content to reiterate the received teaching on God's moral governance of the world as a datum of personal experience for the individual who lives by faith and puts his trust in God (e.g. 2: 7–11; 16: 6–23).

Ben Sira agrees with Qoheleth on one point at least, namely, the exclusion of any form of belief in a life after death as bearing on the intractable problem of the suffering of the innocent. In this respect both adumbrate the Sadducee position in contrast with Pharisee teaching on the resurrection of the dead. The same position seems to be implied in a saying attributed to the sage Antigonus of Sokho— a contemporary or near-contemporary of Ben Sira—recorded in the tractate *Pirke Aboth* of the Mishnah:

Be not like servants who serve the Master on condition of receiving a gift; but be like servants who serve the Master not on condition of receiving a gift. And let the fear of heaven be on you.   (1: 3)

Ben Sira was a scribe, a teacher who conducted his own academy, presumably in Jerusalem (51: 23), and presumably for upper-class youth who aspired to public service. He comes from a time when the sapiential and legal tradition were fully integrated, and as a sage versed in both he set out in his book to synthesize the essence of the Jewish literary tradition in a form both acceptable to observant Jews and intelligible to those acclimatized to the Hellenistic culture of the Ptolemies and Seleucids. This is not the place for a detailed study of his thinking, but we can say that he takes a middle position between religious conservatism and accommodation to Hellenistic culture, leaning more in the direction of the former than the latter.

Two or three decades after Ben Sira wrote his book, however, the Seleucid king Antiochus IV Epiphanes launched his 'final solution of the Jewish problem' (167 BCE), as a result of which such a position became much more difficult to sustain. The persecution began with the proscription of Torah and the establishment of the cult of Zeus in the Jerusalem temple—in effect, with the abolition of the Jewish religion. The ensuing massacre of Jews who remained faithful to the traditional religion—recorded in 1 and 2 Maccabees and reflected in Daniel—raised the problem of divine justice in a more critical way than ever before. It is therefore not surprising that Daniel, written during the crisis to sustain the faith of those suffering persecution, should speak of a final deliverance when those who had died would awake and shine like the brightness of the firmament (Dan. 12: 2–3). The same solution to the problem of overwhelming and apparently triumphant evil is offered in the martyr legends in 2

Maccabees (6: 18–7: 42; 14: 37–46). This should not be thought of as an other-worldly solution to an otherwise insoluble problem, but rather an affirmation that, contrary to all appearances, evil and injustice will not have the last word.

The danger of simply denying death, and therefore bypassing the problem which Qoheleth spent a lifetime trying unsuccessfully to solve, is apparent in The Wisdom of Solomon, a treatise written in Greek in Egypt, probably in the late first century BCE. True to the tradition of scribal piety in which he stands, the author contrasts the fate of the wicked—in this case apostate Jews—with that of the righteous (1–5), emphasizes the reality of divine judgement (e.g. 11: 15–20), and argues that the suffering of the just is a form of divine discipline (3: 6; 16: 5–14). The new element is the Platonic doctrine of the pre-existence and immortality of souls (2: 23–4; 8: 19–20) leading to an emphasis on spiritual rather than physical death. The just only *seem* to die; in reality they live on immortal and reign with God:

> The souls of the righteous are in the hands of God,
> and no torment will ever touch them,
> In the eyes of the foolish they seemed to have died,
> and their departure was thought to be a disaster,
> and their going from us to be their destruction;
> but they are at peace. (3: 1–3)

While belief in life after death, in whatever form it is proposed, cannot be considered a completely satisfactory solution to the problem of theodicy and the divine governance of the world, it has often served as such throughout Christian history. The author of The Wisdom of Solomon has something of value to say, and he is among the first to say it, but it is well that other voices can speak to us out of that tradition, including the authors of Job and Ecclesiastes.

The first two centuries of Roman rule in Palestine, from Pompey's entrance into Jerusalem in 63 BCE to the bloody suppression of the Bar Kochba revolt in 135 CE, were marked by crisis and suffering unparalleled, until this century, in the long continuum of Jewish history. Towards the beginning of this period an author, writing under the pseudonym of Baruch, Jeremiah's scribe, spoke for all his people when he prayed, 'Lord Almighty, God of Israel, the soul in anguish and the wearied spirit cry out to thee' (Baruch 3: 1). In general, however, he follows the Deuteronomic theology according to which Israel is rightly punished for its sins, and specifically for neglecting the prophetic warnings. The second destruction of Jerusalem and its temple in 70 CE precipitated a crisis of faith similar to the first and evoked a passionate search for answers reflected in the literature of that time and the years following. Towards the end of the century an apocalyptic book, appearing under the name of a certain Salathiel, identified with Ezra, struggled with the theological problem of why Israel was destined for so much suffering while the nations which oppressed her went unpunished (2 Esd. 3: 28–36). The first answer, given by the angel Uriel in a vision, appealed to divine transcendence rather like the answer Job received in the whirlwind. On this occasion, however, the questioner was not to be satisfied without further probing:

Why have I been endowed with the power of understanding? For I did not wish to inquire about the ways above, but about those things which we daily experience.   (4: 22)

His insistence brought forth a range of alternative explanations: that the present evil age is drawing to a close (the answer of apocalyptic); that, in spite of appearances to the contrary, God still loves his people; that the course of history is predetermined; finally, that suffering is the essential prelude to a blessed immortality (4: 26–37; 5: 40; 6: 1–6; 7: 14). It is safe to assume that the apocalyptic sage's argument with Uriel represents a lively and passionate debate which was going on among scribes and religious leaders at that time.

The question about divine justice and the moral order of the world raised by the sages of Israel, sharpened by the experience of individual and national suffering and disaster, debated with the greatest freedom in the schools, was therefore by no means put to rest by assurances of a blessed hereafter, in whatever form these may have been offered. It is safe to say that the texts discussed in this chapter, whatever their intellectual limitations, take account of most of the theological options, and that little essential has been added to them in the subsequent centuries. That the problem remains with us is, of course, self-evident. If proof is needed, the reaction to the destruction of a great part of European Judaism in the present century would suffice to show that the responsibility to make sense theologically of 'those things that we daily experience' is not so easily absolved.

4

The Growth of Israel's Legal Tradition

Ordering life by law

The previous chapters have shown how Israelite wisdom aimed at promoting order and maintaining an ethical consensus in the society based on the accumulated experience of the past. In view of this emphasis on justice and order, it would be natural to expect many points of contact with Israel's legal tradition in the different stages of its development and, in doing so, to bring out the different ways in which law and wisdom are related and how they should eventually come together.

Pointing in this direction is the fact that the Hebrew word *torah*, generally translated 'law', more properly stands for teaching or instruction. In Old Testament usage, one speaks of the *torah* of a parent, priest, teacher, or anyone qualified to instruct others. In the course of time, however, the word came to refer to the entire legal heritage of Judaism. According to the traditional Jewish view, this includes not only the law written and delivered at Sinai but also enactments transmitted orally from Moses through various intermediaries to the rabbinic leadership. With the passing of time this oral law, inevitably, came to be written down, and the result was the Mishnah, a substantial corpus of legal material, attributed to Judah the Patriarch, which was compiled towards the end of the second century CE. The process did not, however, stop there, since the Mishnah continued to be expanded and commented on, the final product being the Talmud. In its shorter Palestinian and longer Babylonian versions, this immense collection of legal and narrative material was essentially complete by the fifth century CE. While the word *torah* continued to be used of Pentateuchal law, and of the Pentateuch as a whole, it can also refer in Judaism to the entire corpus of written and (originally) oral law.

The Jewish tradition of referring to the first five books of the Bible as Torah, or 'the five fifths of the Torah', raises an issue which has some relevance for our present theme. For, in spite of the great number of laws which they contain (the traditional count is 613), these books would more naturally be construed as a narrative running from creation to the death of Moses. We need not go into the origin of this practice of referring to a narrative work as 'law' or 'instruction', attested in early Christian writings and in Josephus, except to say that it occurs unequivocally no earlier than the second century BCE. It focuses our attention on the narrative context in which the laws are presented and, more specifically, it suggests that the significance and function of the laws are to be understood in the light of historical events, and especially the history of God's dealings with his people. If, moreover, both law and narrative can together be described as *torah*, in the sense of teaching or instruction, a further implication would be that the law is, in a certain sense, subsumed under wisdom. Thus the teacher Ben Sira, writing about 180 BCE, describes the Jewish philosopher—the seeker after wisdom—as in the first place a student of the law (Ecclus. 39: 1). In a passage which will be discussed in the last chapter of this book, he goes further and identifies the law as divine wisdom sent down to earth to instruct humankind (24: 1–29). When his grandson came to write an introduction to the book about half a century later, he remained true to this perspective by describing the law as the first and principal part of Israel's intellectual heritage.

Writings which have survived from the Second Temple period, whether biblical texts such as Chronicles and Psalms or post-biblical writings such as Jubilees and the Qumran scrolls, testify to the central place of Torah in Jewish intellectual life, private piety, and public worship; and so it has remained to the present. Psalm 1, composed as a prologue to the Psalter, declares happy those whose delight is in the law of Yahweh. The author of Psalm 19 uses a variety of synonyms to describe the effects of the study and observance of Torah:

> The law of Yahweh is perfect,
>   reviving the soul;
> The decrees of Yahweh are sure,
>   making wise the simple;
> The precepts of Yahweh are right,
>   rejoicing the heart;
> The commandment of Yahweh is clear,
>   enlightening the eyes.   (Ps. 19: 7–8)

Torah, in other words, is a sure guide for living not only well and wisely but with joy and deep contentment. Though well known, this should be emphasized precisely because it has been so subject to misunderstanding by Christians. Whether in terms of the sharp contrast between law and gospel, or between 'dead works' and justification by faith, the peculiar Jewish concern to regulate life by law has been, until fairly recently, routinely misrepresented in Christian scholarship as legalism—what Julius Wellhausen a century ago dismissed as a 'petty scheme of salvation'. A concern for law can, certainly, degenerate into legalism and formalism, but such a tendency is a universal temptation, and is found in Christian thought and practice, as much as it is in Judaism.

The concentration on Torah which pervades the piety of Second Temple Judaism can be traced back, in good part, to Deuteronomy. As we shall see later in this chapter, this book represents, in this respect as in others, the great divide between Israel and Judaism. Most critical scholars connect it in some way with movements of reform during the last century of the Kingdom of Judah, and especially during the reign of Josiah (640–609 BCE), the last significant king of Judah, with further expansions and additions from the time of the Babylonian exile and probably later still. In Deuteronomy the word *torah* is used for the first time not of an individual stipulation of law, as previously, but of a collection or corpus of laws (1: 5; 4: 44; etc.). Understood in this sense, *torah* is for Israel the counterpart of the intellectual traditions, the 'wisdom', of other nations:

See, just as Yahweh my God has charged me, I now teach you statutes and ordinances . . . You must observe them diligently, for this will show your wisdom and discernment to the peoples, who, when they hear all these statutes, will say, 'Surely this great nation is a wise and discerning people!'   (Deut. 4: 5–6)

The speaker here addresses his contemporaries in the persona of Moses addressing the Israelites at the end of their trek through the wilderness, but he does so in the manner of the sage addressing his students. We note, too, how the author sees life made up of choices and decisions. He can therefore present the law, in the context of the teaching of the Two Ways, as a guide to choosing and deciding well:

See, I have set before you this day life and prosperity, death and adversity. If you obey the commandments of Yahweh your God that I am commanding you today . . . then you shall live and become numerous.

(30: 15–16)

That throughout the book the speaker is Moses is also a constant reminder to the audience that this wisdom is associated with the memory of events to which Israel owes its existence as a people.

This last point is important for understanding law as the means of defining the kind of community Israel was meant from the beginning to be. Deuteronomy is presented to the reader as the valedictory of Moses, an address delivered to the people in the wilderness on the last day of his life, immediately prior to their entry into Canaan. The book, however, contains many indications, of which the account of Moses' death and burial in the last paragraph is the most obvious, that in its present form it cannot have come from his hand. In the course of this address 'Moses' presents to the assembly what is generally described as a law code, but which is more a programme for life in the land based on a collection of laws (chs. 12–26). We shall see that the Deuteronomic laws are later than the collection of laws in Exodus 20–3, the so-called Covenant Code, and in some respects clearly intended to supersede them. Exodus 20: 24–5, for example, assumes that animal sacrifice may be carried out at different places so long as the altar is constructed in a certain way. Deuteronomy 12: 5–14, on the other hand, stipulates that only at the one place designated by God, which we know corresponds to Jerusalem, is sacrifice legitimate. In due course we shall see other examples. Since laws are generally meant to correspond to actual situations, and since these situations are subject to change with the passing of time, a development in the substance and wording of laws is no more than we would expect. In Israel, however, the acknowledgement of change and adaptation was always tempered by the need to relate law *as a totality* to certain past events in which the community discerned the presence and action of God. Hence all the laws, whenever actually drafted and promulgated, have been back-dated to the great time in the past when Israel stood at Sinai, jour-neyed forty years in the wilderness, and made a new covenant in Moab east of the Jordan as they prepared to enter the Promised Land.

The Israelite stopover at Sinai (referred to also as Horeb) occurs in the course of the wandering in the wilderness of Sinai on the way from Egypt to Canaan. It occupies rather more than a fifth of the entire length of the Pentateuch (Exodus 19: 1—Num. 10: 28) yet lasts only about one year out of the 2,706 which, according to the biblical chronology, elapse between creation and the death of Moses. In the course of this short period of time the decalogue is promul-gated to the entire assembly, the Covenant Code is communicated privately to Moses,with a view to later promulgation, and in a vision on the mountain he receives detailed specifications for the construc-tion of a mobile sanctuary and the setting up of the cult to be car-ried out in it. Other regulations are given and decisions made, many of a cultic nature, in the course of the remaining years in the Sinai wilderness. Then, after arrival in Moab just east of the Jordan, a new covenant is made and a new law given, as presented in Deuteron-omy, on the last day of the life of Moses.

It will be understood that this account of what transpired in 'that great and terrible wilderness' is a literary and theological construct built up over a long period of time with the purpose of authorizing Israel's civic and religious institutions and expressing what was thought to be essential for its identity. It was common practice in ancient and not so ancient times, among the Greeks and Romans for example, to express the essential character of a people in an account of national origins. As we proceed with our enquiry, we shall see that the account inscribes, in both law and narrative, more than one understanding of how Israel is to worship God, regulate its common life, and relate to outsiders.

We note that there are other narrative traditions about the wilder-ness journey which make no mention of the giving of the law at Sinai. Numbers 33, for example, presents an itinerary in the form of a list of stopping places or stages of the trek through the wilderness;

the wilderness of Sinai occurs as the fifteenth, but there is no mention of Moses and the law. Or, again: in the course of negotiating with an Ammonite ruler, Jephthah, one of the 'judges', gives him an account of the Israelite journey out of Egypt which ends at the great oasis of Kadesh. He not only does not mention Sinai, but gives the distinct impression that Kadesh was the goal of the journey from the start (Judg. 11: 14–18). It has also been noticed that in the earliest allusions to Sinai, in poems generally thought to be quite ancient (Deut. 33: 2; Judg. 5: 5; Ps. 68: 9,18), the name is never connected with the giving of the law.

Impressed by these data, some biblical scholars have argued that the entire Sinai–Horeb story has been, so to speak, spliced into an early version of Israelite origins. According to this version the Israelites, after leaving Egypt, stayed a long time at the oasis of Kadesh (as Deut. 1: 46 states), long enough to require the promulgation of laws and the administration of justice based on them. This submerged Kadesh tradition has, however, left only faint traces in the literature (Exod. 18: 13–27; Num. 11: 10–17, 24–30; Deut. 33: 8–11). It is not to our purpose to decide on the merits of this Kadesh hypothesis, but it will serve to remind us that the narrative as we have it is the result of a long process of formation. To convince oneself of this, it will be enough to read the Sinai story and note how often Moses goes up and down the mountain or, alternatively, one might read the account of the conclusion of the law-giving in Exodus 24, noting different answers to the questions of where it takes place, how it is done, and who takes part in it.

A final note on the relation between the events at Sinai–Horeb and those that transpired at the end of the wilderness trek in the land of Moab. According to one strand of the narrative, it appears that at Sinai Yahweh gave the entire law to Moses, who at once promulgated it (Exod. 19: 7–8; 24: 3). This strand is, however, juxtaposed with another according to which only the Ten Commandments were promulgated there and then (Exod. 20: 1, cf. Deut. 4: 10; 5: 4–5, 22), while the detailed stipulations of law were communicated to Moses alone, with the understanding that he would promulgate them at a later time (Exod. 20: 21; 24: 7). The author of Deuteronomy has exploited this delay in order to present an updated version of these stipulations, in the context of a new covenant, designed ostensibly for life in the land which they were about to enter, but in reality for the new situation which confronted Israel at the time when Deuteronomy was written.

Law in early Israel

In its several redactions Deuteronomy represents a landmark in the development and consolidation of Israel's legal traditions. As noted earlier, it marks the watershed between Israel and early Judaism. Probing behind Deuteronomy with a view to reconstructing earlier stages in this development is, unfortunately, no easy task and much will remain uncertain and subject to revision. The reasons can be easily stated. The early history of Israel, in the pre-state period and the beginnings of the monarchy, corresponding to Iron Age I (*c.*1200–1000 BCE), is very obscure and in dispute at the moment, with the result that few statements one might make today about Israelite origins would pass unchallenged. The biblical traditions themselves, therefore, are difficult to 'decode', and, despite confident assertions from some quarters, the archaeological record is no less subject to debate.

With this cautionary proviso, we can say that Israel first appears on the screen of history as a peasant society of villages and settlements organized on real or fictive kinship lines. As elsewhere around the Mediterranean rim, these early Israelites engaged primarily in agricultural pursuits and raising livestock, they were for the most part non-literate, and their way of life called for little occupational diversification. The basic unit was the individual household (*bet 'ab*) composed typically of an extended three-generational family and, if its economic assets permitted it, several dependents, e.g. unmarried relatives, the families of grown children, a divorced adult daughter who had returned to her family of origin, servants and slaves. The intermediate kinship unit was the clan (*mishpaḥah*) composed of a number of households and held together by annual reunions including sacrifice. The macro-unit was the tribe (*shebeṭ, maṭṭeh*) made up of several clans all claiming descent from a real or fictitious ancestor.

Within the extended household the male parent or paterfamilias had considerable but not absolute discretionary power in regulating the lives of members of his extended family and dependents. In some respects his position was comparable to that of the elder or *mukhtar* in a Palestinian Arab village today. In due course, as the state encroached on the kinship network and took over many of its social functions, especially its judicial functions, the authority of the pater-familias was considerably restricted, e.g. in such matters as the treatment of ungovernable sons (Deut. 21: 18–21) and disputes concerning marriage and property. In matters concerning the entire kinship group, however, decisions were in the hands of tribal elders to whom administration of the customary law of the group, orally transmitted, was entrusted. It seems reasonable to assume that something like this mode of organization, which has survived down to the present in traditional societies, obtained in early Israel.

Some of the most primitive features of the administration of justice in Israel reflect the situation obtaining before the formation of the state, e.g. the blood feud and the principle of corporate liability. The former is exemplified by the savage chant of Lamech, descendant of Cain, in Genesis 4: 23–4:

> I have killed a man for wounding me,
>   a young man for striking me.
> If Cain is avenged sevenfold,
>   truly Lamech seventy-sevenfold!

The principle of corporate liability, which gradually lost its place in the administration of justice, with the exception of special cases such as undetected homicide, is reflected in the old formula about God visiting the iniquity of the fathers on the children to the third and fourth generation (Exod. 34: 7; Num. 14: 18). With the passing of time such ideas and formulations inevitably underwent modification. The law of talion (an eye for an eye, a tooth for a tooth, etc.) is best explained as an attempt to control indiscriminate vengeance on the part of the blood-group by applying the principle of equity—in the sense of *only* an eye for an eye, *only* a tooth for a tooth. Since it is found in the Code of Hammurapi and even in Roman law it is not a peculiar feature of Israelite judicial practice.

Practices associated with the blood feud survived only in special applications of the law of sanctuary, dealing with homicide (Num. 35: 16–21; Deut. 19: 12–13), a good example of the state taking over from the kinship system. By the time of Deuteronomy, the group was held responsible only in the exceptional cases of idolatry and homicide (Deut. 13: 6–11; 21: 1–9). Significantly, both deal with acts done in secret when, therefore, the perpetrator cannot be identified. We must bear in mind that we are dealing with a society with no police force and no organized means of detecting and apprehending the criminal. The idea of collective guilt was eventually repudiated as inconsistent with the individual's claim to justice: 'parents shall not be put to death for the children, nor shall children be put to death for their parents; only for their own crimes may persons be put to death' (Deut. 24: 16, cf. 2 Kgs. 14: 6 and Jer. 31: 29). We saw earlier how the Decalogue reflects this advance by limiting the extent of culpability along the line of generations to 'those who hate me' (Exod. 20: 5; Deut. 5: 9).

In a broader sense, early Israel, whatever its remote origins, was a traditional society, which implies that norms for conduct were determined by appeal to the wisdom of the group accumulated over centuries. Here, too, analogy may be a useful means of understanding how a legal tradition and judicial procedures develop in this kind of social context. Among the Ibo of Nigeria, for example, disputes in law are settled by tribal elders dressed for the occasion in the robes and masks of ancestor-spirits; while among the neighbouring Anang tribe the timely citing of a proverbial saying during a judicial hearing can have a decisive effect. The reader will find excellent examples in the works of the Nigerian novelist Chinua Achebe. While the cultures are, of course, widely different, in Israel too the elders, as the depositories of tribal wisdom, played a decisive role in legal matters. They were the ones deemed best able to judge what kind of conduct was or was not consonant with the inherited ethos of the group. The typical form of case law, which states the facts of the case in the protasis ('when a man does x') and the legal consequences in the apodosis ('then y must happen'), is really a case of group experience applied to the solution of specific problems. In this respect it is analogous to those proverbial sayings discussed in a previous chapter in which, as experience teaches, certain consequences are seen to flow from certain behaviours. In such a society, then, law may be described as a specialization of tribal wisdom.

Archaic features are also apparent in the formulation of legal principles which originated in an oral culture. Such, for example, is the sentence of law in Genesis 9: 6 which, literally translated, runs as follows:

> The shedder of the blood of a man—
> By a man his blood shall be shed.

Similar in form are those death penalty sentences which designate the subject with the participle:

Whoever strikes [literally, 'the one striking'] a man so that he dies shall be put to death . . .
Whoever strikes his father or his mother shall be put to death.
Whoever steals [kidnaps] a man . . . shall be put to death.
Whoever curses his father or mother shall be put to death.

(Exod. 21: 12–17)

This too is an ancient formulation which has found its place in the earliest extant collection of Israelite laws (Exod. 20: 23—23: 19). It is, of course, quite different from the case law referred to a moment ago since it enunciates a general principle which is to be applied, with the necessary clarifications and distinctions, to specific cases. We shall see that it belongs to the same class of categoric legal statement as the more familiar 'you shall not kill' type of formulation in the Decalogue.

If, as noted above, case or common law based on precedent is in some respects comparable with proverbial wisdom, categoric law exemplified in the Decalogue has analogies with the admonitions and instructions of the sages. In a previous chapter we saw how the instruction makes frequent use of the imperative: 'Do not plan harm against your neighbour . . . Do not quarrel with anyone without cause . . . Do not envy the violent . . .' (Prov. 3: 29–31). While the grammatical form of the imperative in the Decalogue is not quite identical in Hebrew, the similarity between this kind of admonition and the negative commandments of the Decalogue has led several scholars to suggest that the 'ten words' also derive from the ancient deposit of tribal wisdom and embody the ethos of the kinship group. This may be true in a very general way, but the hypothesis would in any case have to allow for further elaborations and developments. Some of these we shall see at a later point in the chapter.

The Covenant Code: Exodus 20: 23—23: 19

The oldest collection of Israelite laws, described later in the narrative as the 'book of the covenant' (Exod. 24: 7), is presented as given to Moses at Sinai. It is widely agreed, however, that since it presupposes an agrarian economy, it cannot be earlier than the settlement in Canaan, and we have seen that it predates the laws in Deuteronomy. (Note, for example, how many of the case laws it contains have to do with farm animals such as oxen, sheep, and donkeys). It is even possible that many of its stipulations were borrowed from Canaanite common law, though unfortunately no such laws have survived. Moreover, the cultic laws which stand at the beginning and end of the 'code' are, if anything, anti-Canaanite; a circumstance which has suggested to some scholars a connection with the anti-Canaanite and anti-Baalist activities of such early prophets as Elijah and Elisha and the kings of the Northern Kingdom whom they supported.

An alternative and older view maintains that these were the laws proclaimed as part of a covenant ceremony at Shechem, an important centre in the pre-state period, about forty miles due north of Jerusalem (Josh. 8: 30–5; 24: 1–28, cf. Deut. 27). Those who accept this view conclude that the Covenant Code was the law for the tribal federation centred on the Shechem sanctuary in the period preceding the rise of the monarchy. The problem is that the entire issue of the existence, origin, and make-up of such a tribal structure as the *Sitz im Leben* of early Israelite law in the pre-state period, once thought to be definitively solved, is now once more called in question.

We can at least be tolerably certain that this collection existed independently prior to its incorporation into the Sinai narrative in Exodus 20–3. The juxtaposition of different kinds of legal material in it makes it equally clear that it reached its present form only after a considerable passage of time. First, cultic laws governing idolatry, the construction of altars, and sacrifice precede the title at Exod. 21: 1 ('these are the ordinances . . .'), the collection ends with cultic legislation (23: 10–19), and a solemn *religious* prohibition stands at the centre—'whoever sacrifices to any god, other than Yahweh alone, shall be devoted to destruction' (22: 20). This arrangement of brack-eting or ring composition and pivoting on a central point suggests the intent of providing a civic code with a religious framework, implying the conviction that societal relations depend on first defin-ing the society's proper relationship to God. The law is a law for *this* community, defining the kind of community it is meant to be. It will be seen, further, that the laws are not all of a kind. The death penalty sentences in the participial form, presented earlier, interrupt a series of miscellaneous case laws or ordinances (21: 1—22: 17) which are quite different in form from the series of laws in the imperative which follows (22: 18—23: 19). Since case law (the term 'casuistic' is also often used) is the standard form of legal enactment in Israel and the ancient Near East, the ancestor of our common law, it is rea-sonable to infer that the sixteen laws of this kind with their explana-tory codicils formed a separate collection illustrative of early Israelite common law.

The second half of the Code, excluding the concluding ritual laws, is in some respects quite different (Exod. 22: 21—23: 19). Most of the stipulations are of the apodictic kind ('you shall not . . .'), and it is only here that motivation is provided for the observance of the laws. All of the laws at Sinai are presented as enunciated by Yahweh (following on the introduction in Exod. 20: 1), but only in this sec-tion of the Covenant Code is it clear that God is speaking. Note, too, that this last segment begins and ends with a law enjoining care for the resident alien, suggesting that this point of law, reinforced by collective memory of alien status in Egypt, is in some way indicative of the character and intent of the laws as a whole.

As to the character of Israelite law in general: until the beginning of this century the laws in the Old Testament were the only ones known to us from the ancient Near East. It was therefore impossi-ble to assess the claims made by both Jews and Christians, for exam-ple, that biblical law was uniquely humanitarian in character or inspired by a high ideal of justice unattested elsewhere. The absence of comparative material also made it very difficult to get a precise idea of the form and function of the different kinds of legal mater-ial found in the Old Testament. Then, during the winter of 1901/2 the French archaeologist Jacques de Morgan discovered in the Elamite city of Susa (Shushan) the stele (now in the Louvre) inscribed with the laws of Hammurapi the king of Babylon. These 282 case laws, introduced by a prologue and rounded out with an epilogue praising the king as guardian of justice, were engraved near the beginning of Hammurapi's reign (*c.*1728–1686 BCE). They almost certainly draw on a legal tradition of even greater antiquity, and were very influential in perpetuating that tradition.

In the intervening years a good cross-section of legal material has come to light from Mesopotamia and Asia Minor, most of which dates from the second millennium BCE or earlier. This includes fragmentary law collections from Sumerian cities, Hittite and Assyrian laws from the fourteenth and twelfth centuries respectively, and Neo-Babylonian laws from the sixth century BCE, the only ones more recent than several of the Israelite laws. While in no case is it possible to derive Israelite law directly from this mostly earlier material, it is now quite clear that early Israel inherited a legal tradition which can be traced back to Mesopotamia of the third and second millennium BCE.

An interesting feature of several of these collections, including the laws of Hammurapi, is that they are provided with a prologue and epilogue. The laws of Ur-Nammu, founder of the third dynasty of Ur towards the end of the third millennium BCE, are introduced by an address of the king listing the benefits he had conferred on his people, of which the most important was maintaining justice and protecting the disadvantaged:

The orphan was not delivered up to the rich man,
The widow was not delivered up to the mighty man,
The man of one shekel was not delivered up to the man of one mina.

(lines 162–8)

The same kind of statement occurs as a preface to the laws of Lipit-ishtar of the Sumerian city of Isin and, at greater length, in the prologue to the laws of Hammurapi. In addition, the last two are rounded off with an epilogue which stipulates the setting up of the stele on which the laws were written and enjoins that all are to have free access to it. The code of Hammurapi also prohibits any alteration to the laws and ends with curses and blessings to ensure that they are respected and obeyed.

The laws in the Old Testament, and especially those in

Deuteronomy, are also provided with such prefaces and conclusions. The most obvious difference is that the Israelite laws are presented within a continuous historical context, implying that it is this history which gives the law its meaning for Israel.

A study of the Mesopotamian laws also raises the difficult question of the nature, origin, and function of such collections. The term 'law code' is widely used, but if by this designation we mean something analogous to the Napoleonic Code it would clearly be inappropriate. None of the collections, not even that of Hammurapi with its 282 paragraphs, covers all significant aspects of public life or even comes close to being comprehensive. The sixteen paragraphs of the Covenant Code (Exod. 21: 1–11, 18–36; 22: 1–17), even when augmented with the categoric statements about cult and other matters, cover only a small area of public life. Nowhere in the Old Testament, for example, do we find laws regulating marriage or legislating on divorce—who may initiate it, under what circumstances, and with what consequences. Some have thought that the purpose of the collections was to provide guidance for magistrates on more difficult and problematic cases of law. But this is hardly the solution, since most of the situations covered are not particularly difficult. Perhaps, then, we can go back to our original point about the confluence of the sapiential–didactic and legal traditions, and suggest that the writing down of the laws, and especially the provision of motivation for their observance, was intended as another form of moral guidance and instruction, comparable to the collection of aphoristic material in the Book of Proverbs.

With regard to the Mesopotamian collections, it has also been suggested that they were compiled from royal edicts issued at the beginning of a reign or at seven-year intervals during it. Such edicts, like that of a later king of Babylon named Ammisaduqa which is still extant, dealt only with exceptional matters such as the manumission of slaves and the forgiveness of debts. This will remind us of the Old Testament laws governing the sabbatical and jubilee years (Exod. 23: 10–11; Lev. 25) and the stipulation that the law be read publicly every seven years (Deut. 31: 10–13). It is also worth noting that the practice of reissuing and revalidating laws at the beginning of a reign continued down into the Persian period.

Whatever their origin, these collections of laws would have passed eventually under the control of scribes and scholars who assumed responsibility for their interpretation. Evidence of the activity of these legal scholars can be seen in the amplifications of the individual laws in the Covenant Code. Some of these expansions are primarily explanatory, others motivational. Take, for example, the law which stipulates that a creditor must return a garment taken in pledge between sundown and sunrise (expansion in italics):

If you take your neighbour's cloak in pawn, you shall restore it before the sun goes down; *for it may be your neighbour's only clothing to use as cover; in what else shall that person sleep? And if your neighbour cries out to me, I will listen, for I am compassionate.* (Exod. 22: 26–7)

In other cases the expansion provides motivation either of a general ethical kind or by reference to specifically Israelite traditions. An example such as the resident alien law provides an important clue to the relationship between the laws and the narrative tradition, especially since, as we saw earlier, it brackets the second part of the Covenant Code:

You shall not wrong or oppress a resident alien, *for you were aliens in the land of Egypt.* (Exod. 22: 21)

You shall not oppress a resident alien; *you know what it means to be an alien* [literally: you know the heart of an alien], *for you were aliens in the land of Egypt.* (Exod. 23: 9)

A comparison of the laws in the Mesopotamian collections with those of the Covenant Code does not support the view that the latter are in all respects more advanced and humanitarian in character. Nor does it substantiate the liberal idea of a progressively more enlightened approach to penal legislation. The death penalty occurs more often in early Israelite legislation, for example, than in the Sumerian laws where capital sentence is reserved to the crown. In the laws of Eshnunna, the owner of a rogue ox which kills someone is fined, whereas in the Covenant Code he is sentenced to death (Exod. 21: 29). The Code of Hammurapi provides better protection to a woman divorced by her husband than does early Israelite legislation, and stipulates that the insolvent person taken into indentured service has to be freed after three years rather than six, as in the early Israelite law (Exod. 21: 2). The Covenant Code stands apart not so much by virtue of its substance, but because of the historical-narrative context in which it is presented and its evolution, seen especially in the expansions, towards a more comprehensive guide for living.

In point of fact, the relative degree of enlightenment reflected in laws is generally a function of the stage of social and political evolution reached by a society in which the laws are in force. In societies which still preserve a tribal structure, for example, a case of homicide is generally settled by blood feud. In this respect early Israel is not very different from the society reflected in the Homeric poems. With the passage from tribal society to state, however, law codes and judicial procedures come into existence which reserve judgement in many important matters to the state. In Mesopotamia this stage of evolution occurred no later than the second millennium, while in Greece we have to wait until the seventh century BCE for the first written state law, that of Draco of Athens, almost exactly contemporary with the promulgation of the Deuteronomic Law in Judah. We have already seen that in Deuteronomy the principle of corporate liability, characteristic of a tribal structure, survives only in the exceptional cases of homicide and apostasy where the perpetrator remains undetected.

We now need to look a little more closely at the way in which the stipulations of the Covenant Code are formulated. The title identifies the case laws as 'ordinances' and the context distinguishes these from the kind of categoric or apodictic statements found in the Decalogue which are called simply 'words' (Exod. 20: 1; 24: 3). The first of the sixteen ordinances provides a good example of how case law was formulated and some indication as to how it was administered. We may set it out as follows:

When you buy a male Hebrew slave, he shall serve six years, but in the seventh he shall go out a free person, without debt.
1. If he comes in single, he shall go out single;
2. If he comes in married, then his wife shall go out with him.
3. If his master gives him a wife and she bears him sons or daughters, the wife and her children shall be her master's and he shall go out alone.
4. But if the slave declares, 'I love my master, my wife, and my children; I will not go out a free person,' then his master shall bring him before God. He shall be brought to the door or the doorpost; and his

master shall pierce his ear with an awl; and he shall serve him for life.
(Exod.21: 2–6)

The protasis gives the facts of the case, i.e., the purchase of a Hebrew slave, and the apodosis the legal consequences, i.e., mandatory release in the seventh year after purchase. As is generally the case, however, special circumstances call for more specific rulings, and these are laid out in subordinate clauses. In this instance there are four: (1) a slave who is single at the time of purchase and remains single; (2) a slave who is married at the time of purchase; (3) one who marries after becoming the property of his master; (4) one in the third category who does not wish to separate from his wife and children. Only this last calls for a special juridical act, since it results legally in a state of perpetual slavery and therefore contradicts the basic intent of the law. A symbolic act must therefore be carried out at the tribal sanctuary ('before God'), or perhaps in front of the household gods, namely, the piercing of the slave's ear as the organ of hearing and obeying. This act, needless to say, was no more cruel than boring a small hole in the ear lobe to fit an ear-ring.

If we compare this ordinance about slaves with the Deuteronomic reformulation (Deut. 15: 12–18) we shall get some idea of the development of the legal tradition in Israel. There is the same basic stipulation, presented under the rubric of the year of release (15: 1), with the interesting exception that the female slave is given explicit mention (vv. 12, 17). The law is now silent on the eventuality of the slave having to choose between his freedom and abandoning his wife and children, since perpetual slavery results only when the slave in question opts to remain out of attachment to his master. It is also stipulated that the master must provide liberally for his manumitted slave in the year of release. Motivation is supplied with reference to Israel's common memory of slavery in Egypt, a feature which is also found in the Covenant Code, as we have seen.

Another example may be given, of some contemporary interest since it is the only biblical legal enactment with any relevance to the moral issue of abortion:

When people who are fighting injure a pregnant woman so that there is a miscarriage, and yet no further harm follows, the one responsible shall be fined what the woman's husband demands, paying as much as the judges determine. If any harm follows, then you shall give life for life, eye for eye, tooth for tooth, hand for hand, foot for foot, burn for burn, wound for wound, stripe for stripe. (21: 22–4)

The situation is a brawl in which a pregnant woman is injured, unintentionally in this case, resulting in miscarriage. The further harm refers not to the foetus but to injury or death suffered by the woman, in which case the law of talion is applied. Otherwise damages for the loss of the foetus are levied, there being some mechanism for negotiation on the basis of the husband's initial demand. There is no sense that the foetus is regarded as a person subject to the protection of the law, but in that society children were a valuable commodity and their loss called for compensation. Surprisingly perhaps, a similar law is found in practically all the collections surviving from the ancient Near East, allowing for a valuable comparativist study.

It was, then, this kind of case law which formed the basis for the daily administration of justice in Israel, as elsewhere in the Near East. From the Old Testament narrative as well as the laws some idea can be formed as to how this operated. We hear frequently of the taking of oaths (crucial in a society without a police force), the role of witnesses, the practice of the ordeal, and the like. Much of the ordinary business of life would be transacted within the household according to the accepted mores of the kinship group. Otherwise, the normal location for such matters as disputes about property, closing deals, witnessing contracts, dealing with various forms of social deviance, was the 'city gate', meaning either the space at the entrance of a village or the plaza which formed an essential part of the gate complex known from the excavation of Bronze Age and Iron Age sites. An example of such transactions occurs towards the end of Ruth when her nearest kinsman is given first refusal of Naomi's property and of the right to marry Ruth which went with it. The text describes the gathering of the principals in the case:

No sooner had Boaz gone up to the gate and sat down there than the next-of-kin, of whom Boaz had spoken, came passing by. So Boaz said, 'Come over, friend; sit down here'; and he went over and sat down. Then Boaz took ten men of the elders of the city, and said, 'Sit down here'; so they sat down. (4: 1–2)

—and so the stage is set for the ensuing negotiations. The elders clearly played an important part in the day-to-day administration of justice, though their authority was counterbalanced and in some respects restricted by state-appointed judges under the monarchy, including a central judiciary or court of appeals in Jerusalem (Deut. 17: 8–13, cf. 2 Chr. 19: 5–11) which claimed exclusive jurisdiction over several important matters, such as false testimony. Allusions in the Pentateuch to Moses subdelegating judicial authority (e.g. Exod. 18: 13–26; Deut. 1: 9–18) no doubt reflect this important institution. True to the ancient Near Eastern ideal of the monarch as the custodian of justice, there was, ideally at least, free access to the king as the final arbiter of disputed cases or of those in which an alleged miscarriage of justice had taken place. We recall the wise woman of Tekoa seeking judicial intervention from David (2 Sam. 14: 4–20) and the case of the newborn child disputed before Solomon by two prostitutes (1 Kgs. 3: 16–28), but to what extent these are representative or even historical we cannot say.

The Decalogue

The Covenant Code contains, in addition to case laws, different kinds of categoric statements, or legal principles and norms, which must now be considered. The so-called 'law of the altar' which prefaces the entire collection (20: 23–6) is, formally, more like an instruction. It contains imperatives, includes a promise of divine blessing, and provides reasons for constructing altars in the traditional way prescribed. It therefore hardly qualifies as law in the strict sense of the term. The death penalty series (21: 12–17) has already been introduced as a distinct kind of categoric or apodictic enactment similar to the curse-formulations occurring elsewhere in the Pentateuch (Deut. 27: 15–26). In the last part of the collection (Exod. 23: 1–19) there is also a prevalence of mixed forms, with commands in the positive and negative, exhortation and motivation, all much more reminiscent of a catechism than a law code.

We saw earlier that the Sinai narrative distinguishes between 'ordinances' (the case laws) and 'words' or 'utterances', and that the Decalogue is introduced as 'words'. It is understood that these 'words' are universally binding and, since they are introduced as divine discourse ('I am Yahweh your God . . .'), they are intended as a direct expression of the will of God for Israel. In Israel and elsewhere, legal and moral principles or norms of this kind are generally presented in series. The Decalogue is only one of several such series of apodictic statements in the Pentateuch. The Covenant Code contains, besides the five formulaic death sentences discussed earlier, a series of commands mostly in the negative (22: 18–23) and a list of prohibitives dealing with the administration of justice (23: 1–3, 6–9), both of which may be derived from originally independent decalogues. The series promulgated after the apostasy of the Golden Calf (34: 13–26) may also have started out as a decalogue, and in the present state of the text is described as such (34: 28), though it now numbers eleven stipulations. Psalm 15 contains a list of ten moral qualifications for taking part in temple worship. The litany of curses which concludes the covenant-making in Deuteronomy (27: 15–26) lists twelve infractions and is therefore a dodecalogue. The practice of listing legal enactments or principles of law in a short series, with a preference for ten or twelve, is therefore well attested and no doubt ancient.

Attempts have been made to identify a model for the Decalogue outside of Israel which might help to solve the much debated problem of its date and origin. Many scholars have been impressed by certain structural similarities between Hittite vassal treaties, discovered at the ancient Hittite capital of Boghazköy near Ankara in Turkey, and the way in which covenants are made and renewed in the Old Testament. Since these treaties date from the fourteenth and thirteenth centuries BCE, the analogy also seemed to have the advantage of confirming the great antiquity of these biblical formulations. The treaties in question begin with a preamble in which the suzerain identifies himself, and continue with an account of past benefits (real or fictitious) conferred on the vassal, obviously with a view to motivating him to remain faithful to his allegiance. There then follow the stipulations of the treaty, sometimes in a form analogous to the apodictic laws, together with provisions for its display and public reading. It concludes with a list of gods as witnesses and a series of blessings and curses contingent on its observance and violation respectively.

Since something of the same structure can be detected in certain Old Testament passages dealing with law and covenant, these treaty texts have been seen to provide some important clues to the origin and date of the Israelite covenant idea. The analogy has certainly proved to be stimulating and valuable, not least in highlighting the political dimension of early Israelite religious thinking, but not all the claims made for it have been sustained. It can be shown, for example, that the structure in question is not confined to Hittite international treaties of the late second millennium but is also a feature of Assyrian treaties roughly contemporary with Jeremiah and the Book of Deuteronomy. Not all the proposed similarities, moreover, hold up under close scrutiny, and certainly not with respect to the Decalogue. The prologue, 'I am Yahweh your God who brought you out of the land of Egypt, out of the house of bondage', is similar in neither form nor length to the preambles and historical introductions to the treaties. It is a self-identification formula and not a historical prologue. The stipulations are also, for the most part, couched in a different way, and there is no parallel in the treaties to the series of ten or twelve.

Other analogies which have been proposed, e.g. lists of misdeeds disavowed by the faithful in the Egyptian Books of the Dead and Assyrian catalogues of sins, are also wide of the mark. We have to conclude that, in the present state of our knowledge, the Decalogue has to be explained as a purely internal, Israelite development, even if we cannot trace that development with any great assurance.

In an important study published in 1934 under the title 'The Origins of Israelite Law', the German scholar Albrecht Alt argued that the categoric or apodictic laws, as distinct from case law, originated in the early Israelite cult of the amphictyony, and were recited during the autumnal festival of Sukkoth (Tabernacles) when the covenant between Yahweh and the people was solemnly renewed. The biblical text does, in fact, attest to the occasional public reading of the law, which was just about the only possible way to promulgate it in a society for the most part illiterate:

Moses commanded them, 'Every seventh year, in the scheduled year of remission, during the festival of booths, when all Israel comes to appear before Yahweh your God at the place that he will choose, you shall read this law before all Israel in their hearing.' (Deut. 31: 10–11)

This practice of public reading continued down into the late biblical period, and is exemplified in the great liturgical assembly led by Ezra during his mission to the province of Judah (Neh. 7: 73—8: 8). One of the major functions of the cult in Israel was to keep on reaffirming the ethical implications of the covenant-relationship. There can be no doubt, then, that the cult incorporated the law in this way, but it is quite another matter to argue that it somehow *generated* this form of legal pronouncement. It seems more likely that several factors have to be reckoned with, cultic recital being only one of them.

A further aspect comes into view when we note that the Decalogue has close affinity with the ethical teaching of the prophets. Where the prophets under the monarchy denounce their contemporaries, their accusations are, for the most part, highly specific. They can also be shown to correspond in many instances to equally specific points of law. When Amos, for example, condemns those who sleep on garments taken in pledge (2: 8) he does not cite but is clearly referring to the law in the Covenant Code, quoted earlier, which obliges a creditor to return a pawned garment between sundown and sunrise (Exod. 22: 26–7). We also detect a generalizing tendency in prophetic preaching whereby the essence of the laws, and of the individual, itemized demands they lay on their contemporaries, is expressed in a brief and compendious way. An example would be the much-quoted text from Micah (6: 8):

> He has told you, O mortal, what is good;
> and what does Yahweh require of you
> but to do justice, and to love kindness,
> and to walk humbly with your God?

When, on the other hand, an equally broad description of a faithless community is called for, we hear unmistakable echoes of the Decalogue:

> There is swearing, lying, killing, stealing and committing adultery;
> they break all bounds and murder follows murder.
> (Hos. 4: 2)

Will you steal, murder, commit adultery, swear falsely, make offerings to Baal, and go after other gods that you have not known, and then come and stand before me in this house? (Jer. 7: 9–10)

This might be thought to imply that the Decalogue was already familiar by the time of the prophets. But in view of the different order in which the offences occur here, together with the fact that all of them can be found in series other than the Decalogue, it seems better to conclude that prophetic preaching influenced the final form of the Decalogue. It may therefore be tentatively proposed that this compendium of the moral life was the result of a selection from older lists which reached its final form in Exodus and Deuteronomy by way of prophetic preaching.

Comparison of the two versions of the Decalogue (Exod. 20: 1–17 and Deut. 5: 6–21) leads to the conclusion that the individual stipulations—all save two of which are in the negative—have been expanded in the course of usage. Thus, the prohibition against making images is rounded off with a theological reason: the exclusive claim which the God of Israel lays on his devotees. The sabbath command is enjoined in one case (Exod. 20: 11) with reference to Creation and in the other (Deut. 5: 14–15) on humanitarian grounds—to provide respite for servants—and with specific reference to the tradition of Israel in Egypt. These contrasting motivations are often thought to reflect the difference between a Priestly (in Exodus) and a Deuteronomic version, but in fact both are unmistakably Deuteronomic in formulation. Motivation is also provided for honouring parents, in both cases to secure lasting possession of the land—a typically Deuteronomic theme. Whatever the original form of the tenth word, it is noticeable that in Deuteronomy the wife is no longer under the rubric of household, but is listed separately— a small step towards acknowledging the dignity of the woman as a person in her own right.

These expansions are also found in the other series and throw valuable light on the way the law functioned in Israel. They help us to understand how biblical law, far from being imposed all at one time by divine dictate, evolved out of the needs and aspirations of a people living in a specific environment and inheriting customs and traditions both indigenous and foreign. They also help to bring out the theological significance of law as related to a certain understanding of the character of Israel's God and the common memory through which Israel affirmed and preserved its identity and way of life.

The Second Law: Deuteronomy, religious programme and civil constitution

In its detailed stipulations, the Covenant Code reflects a society of mostly small farmers and stockbreeders. Its frequent references to slaves, most of whom would be men, women, and children forced by insolvency into indentured service, is only one indication of the hardship endemic to life at that time and in those circumstances. In a subsistence economy of that kind, and in the physical environment of Palestine in which regular rainfall in the winter and early spring was vital to survival, it might only take back-to-back droughts to drive a household into insolvency and eventual disintegration. To this unstable situation we must add the ingredient of almost constant external threat in the form of warfare and consequent social upheaval. Pressure from the Philistine advance into the hill country was followed by the 'little' expansionist wars of David, then fighting between the two kingdoms after the death of Solomon, the Aramean wars, and so on down to the Assyrian conquest in the eighth century BCE.

Noticeably absent from the Covenant Code are references to state officials and the apparatus of state control in general. One law forbids cursing 'a leader of your people' (Exod. 22: 28), but the Hebrew term *nasi* refers, here as elsewhere, not to a monarch but to a tribal official, perhaps a kind of president of the corps of tribal elders. The Deuteronomic law, by contrast, has all the indications of being a state document, and refers to the rights and duties of state officials including the monarch, judges, and clergy. We conclude therefore that it comes from a time when the apparatus of state control was well on its way to supplanting a social form of life based on the kinship and tribal network.

It will not be necessary to trace in detail the process, in many respects still very obscure, by which Israelite and Judean states emerged on Canaanite soil. External pressures, especially from the Philistines who had occupied part of the Palestinian littoral in the eleventh century BCE, also perhaps internal pressures caused by ecological and demographic factors, led to the appointment of *ad hoc* military leaders. These circumstances also created opportunities for the emergence of *condottieri* and brigand chieftains with their own private armies recruited from the disaffected and the dispossessed, a situation well documented in the Book of Judges and the story of David's rise to power. The successive stages are well known from the biblical record. They culminated in the kingdom of David and Solomon, though there are some indications that the apparatus of statehood was not fully in place until somewhat later.

Though the monarchy and its attendant institutions existed theo- retically to support, serve, and enhance the existing tribal organiza- tion and the ethos which sustained it, it soon became clear that this was not going to happen. Whatever its historical character, the story of the seer Nathan taking David to task for adultery (2 Sam. 12: 1–15) reflects the tension inherent in a situation somewhat peculiar to Israel; in one of the great empires no one would have made a song and dance about a ruler possessing the wife of one of his subjects. Tension is also apparent later in the same narrative when Amnon, first in line to succeed David, attempts to seduce his half-sister Tamar and is warned by her that 'such a thing is not done in Israel' (13: 12), implying that this outrage would be a gross violation of the traditional law and ethos of the kinship group. In the following cen- tury Ahab, ruler of the Northern Kingdom, planned to extend the palace grounds in Samaria and, to that end, offered to buy out a landowner who had a vineyard adjacent to the palace. Despite the favourable terms of the contract, the latter refused on the traditional grounds of the inalienability of family property, a decision in which Ahab clearly felt, initially at least, he had no alternative but to acqui- esce (1 Kgs. 21: 1–4). Naboth's probably ill-advised and in the event fatal refusal of the king's offer, and the latter's initial acquiescence in his refusal, would be difficult to parallel in contemporary monar- chies, which of course explains the scornful reaction of Jezebel, accustomed as she was to quite different procedures in the Phoenician cities. The incident attests to the persistence of a tradi- tional legal system, but also to its fragility.

The outcome of the dispute between Ahab and Naboth, with the latter a victim of judicial murder and the former in possession of his subject's property, may serve to show how this situation of tension, left to itself, would tend to be resolved. Inevitably Israel was drawn into conformity with the model of statehood provided by existing city-states in the region, including Jerusalem. Support of a state bureaucracy, which included the cult, and of large-scale building projects, which included a national shrine employing numerous cultic personnel, imposed a severe economic burden on the farming households for whom the Covenant Code was drafted. A standing army took the place of the tribal levy and, together with forced labour, became another source of discontent. Erosion of patrimonial domain by forced purchase, expropriation or enclosure, illustrated by the Naboth incident, posed a direct threat to the basis of a traditional way of life and the ethos which sustained it.

It is against this background, roughly sketched, that we have to assess the social role of those prophets who operated independently of state institutions. A reading of the eighth-century prophets— Hosea and Amos, Micah and Isaiah—will show how often their diatribe is directed against state institutions and the abuse of political and economic power. Together with other groups mentioned here and there in the record (e.g. Nazirites and Rechabites), they represented a conservative reaction to changes which threatened a traditional way of life. Hence the frequent allusion in prophetic books to Israel's origins and the failure of their contemporaries to honour ancient commitments. Hence also their attack on the state cults of both kingdoms as legitimating what they took to be a fundamentally unjust and flawed political and social system. While most of the prophets had very limited success in directly influencing the society of their day, their protest found an at least partial expression in Deuteronomy and in this way was preserved as a normative source of social ethics even after the loss of national independence.

The title of Deuteronomy derives from the Greek *deuteros nomos*, a second law, which in turn derives from Deuteronomy 17: 18 where it is said that the king must write for himself 'a copy of this law' to keep by him. But the book does in fact contain a second law, in so far as several of the stipulations in chapters 12–26, the legal core of the book, represent an updated and revised form of laws in the Covenant Code. The title is therefore not inappropriate, whatever the intentions of the Greek translators may have been. The opening paragraph introduces the book as discourse of Moses: 'These are the words that Moses spoke to all Israel beyond the Jordan . . .' (1: 1); and since he dies on the same day, as recorded in the final chapter, the book can be described as a transcript of his valedictory address, accompanied by the making of a new covenant over and above the Sinai–Horeb covenant (29: 1) and the giving of a new law.

That Deuteronomy was not composed all at one time and by one hand will be obvious already from this opening paragraph (1: 1–5) which has been expanded in different ways in the course of the book's transmission. The addition of topographical detail (vv. 1*b*–2, 4) links that moment in time with the giving of the law at Sinai (here referred to as Horeb) and the even older tradition of judicial activity at the oasis of Kadesh in the Sinai peninsula. The precise date—the first day of the eleventh month of the fortieth year counting from the exodus from Egypt (v. 3)—is characteristic not of Deuteronomy but of the Priestly Source (P). Together with the account of Moses' death at the end of the book (32: 48–52; 34: 1, 7–9), acknowledged to be from the same source, it provides us with a valuable clue to the process (to be discussed in the next chapter) by which Deuteronomy was incorporated into the mainline Priestly narrative of the Pentateuch. Returning to the opening paragraph, we note how Moses is presented as a scribe who undertakes to explain the law (v. 5). We expect him to start doing so at once, but this is only the first of several false starts over eleven chapters before he actually does so. This, then, is one of several indications that the book reached its present form only after a long and complex process of transmission.

We note, too, that the introductory paragraph alludes to a law which requires interpretation (1: 5). The reader is therefore alerted to the fact that the book will contain law together with legal exposition and commentary. That it is attributed to Moses as the direct recipient of commandments of divine origin also indicates its authoritative, we might say its canonical status. The injunction not to add to or subtract from anything in the book (4: 2; 12: 32) is the kind of language associated with canonical texts from the ancient Near East, e.g. copies of international treaties. The requirement that the monarch have his own copy of the law drafted by its official custodians, the levitical priests, points in the same direction (17: 18–19). Like international treaties from that time, it is fortified by blessings and even more by curses (chs. 27–8), and it is to be deposited in a public place and read publicly in solemn assembly at stated intervals (31: 9–13, 24–29).

It seems, then, that the authors of the original version of Deuteronomy were familiar with procedures for drafting international treaties. Assyrian vassal treaties and loyalty oaths extant from that time, the seventh century BCE, exhibit the following components, though not all are present in all cases: a preamble identifies the parties involved in the treaty, and is sometimes accompanied by a brief historical introduction; there follow the stipulations covering obligations of a general nature (e.g. loyalty to the Assyrian king) and detailed requirements (e.g. commercial concessions); these are corroborated by violation clauses and curses which form the very backbone of the treaty, and gods are called to witness the agreement of the two parties. All these elements, with the obvious exception of calling gods to witness (but see 4: 26, 'I call heaven and earth to witness against you today . . .'), are present in Deuteronomy. The book must, then, have been drafted by scribes at the Judean court educated in much the same way as those for whom the aphoristic literature in Proverbs was put together; another indication, therefore, of the close connections between the legal and sapiential–didactic traditions.

Before going further it will be convenient to set out the structure of the book as follows:

1: 1–5	Superscription
1: 6—3: 29	Historical summary: from Horeb to Moab
4: 1–40	Concluding address: lessons from the history
4: 41–3	Appendix: cities of refuge
4: 44–9	Superscription
5	Address of Moses presenting the Decalogue
6–11	Commentary on the first word of the Decalogue
12–26	The Deuteronomic law book
27	Ratification of the covenant
28: 1—29: 1	Blessings and curses
29: 2—30: 20	Final address of Moses
31–4	Conclusion to Deuteronomy and the Pentateuch

We have seen that the superscript (1: 1–5) alerts us to the composite nature of the book, a conclusion confirmed by other indications, e.g., frequent shifts from the singular to the plural. In the opening verses we are promised legal exposition, but there follows instead a

historical summary in the form of personal reminiscence of Moses
(1: 6—3: 29). This covers a sequence of events beginning with the
command to leave Horeb, continuing with the setting up of a judicial system, and describing preliminaries to the occupation of Canaan
which Moses himself was forbidden to enter. A little later we find
another solemn introduction to the law, again with topographical
expansions (4: 44–9), but there follows another homily of Moses in
the course of which the Decalogue is repeated. After one more introduction (6: 1–3), followed by the *shema*, in Judaism still the central
confession of faith, we eventually come to the stipulations (12–26),
but presented in a much more discursive way than the laws in the
Covenant Code or the other Near Eastern compilations. The law
book is rounded off with the ratification of the covenant, blessings
and curses, and a final homily (27–30). In the last section (31–4),
Moses delivers the final charge to Joshua and the people as they prepare to occupy the land. It also contains the finale to the Pentateuch
as a whole, especially apparent in the penultimate statement:

Never since has there arisen a prophet in Israel like Moses, whom
Yahweh knew face to face.   (34: 10)

The intent here is to deny parity between Moses and the prophets
who followed him by putting the mode of revelation proper to Moses
on a quite different and higher level than that of the prophet. After
this closure, we would not anticipate that the Law would be followed
by the Prophets. This, however, is what happened, and, when it happened, the expanded corpus of writings was rounded off with a new
finale:

Remember the teaching of my servant Moses, the statutes and ordinances that I commanded him at Horeb for all Israel.
Lo, I will send you the prophet Elijah before the great and terrible day
of Yahweh comes . . .   (Mal. 4: 4–5)

While it is no longer possible to reconstruct precisely the stages
by which the book reached its present form, there is broad agreement that an earlier version began with the introduction at 4: 44,
included most of 4: 44—11: 32 and of the legal material in 12–26,
and ended with the long list of curses in chapter 28 and the solemn
finale at 29: 1 ('These are the words of the covenant . . .'). The

reader can test for the presence of successive editing by noting how Levites function in the covenant-making in chapter 27: levitical priests assist Moses (v. 9), Levites, as an order distinct from priests, pronounce the curses (v. 14), and the tribe of Levi takes its place on Mount Gerizim (v. 12). That an original version was expanded during the Babylonian exile is suggested by the frequent allusions to exile in 4: 1–40 and chapters 29–30. These sections read rather like sermons delivered to the Jewish communities in the Babylonian or Egyptian diaspora in which the homilist works the themes of seeking God, returning to him, the circumcision of the heart, and the assurance of an eventual ingathering in the land (4: 29–31; 30: 1–10). There is also this difference, that now curse and blessing are seen not as simultaneous alternatives but successive stages, thereby holding out hope for the future.

Critical study of the book got off to a promising start at the beginning of the nineteenth century when Wilhelm de Wette noted and commented on the correspondence between the religious reforms of Josiah (640–609 BCE), as described in 2 Kings 23, and the cultic legislation in Deuteronomy. The historian's account of the reforms give us a fair idea of the religious situation in Judah around the middle of the seventh century BCE: the Canaanite deities Baal and Asherah worshipped in the Jerusalem temple, male cult prostitutes employed in the temple precincts, non-Yahwistic priests sacrificing to pagan deities on the 'high places' around the country, children offered to Molech in the tophet south of Jerusalem. The historian informs us that the reforms were set in motion by the finding of a law book during repair work on the temple during the eighteenth year of the king's reign (2 Kgs. 22: 8). But the very fact of repairing the temple points to a movement of religious renewal already under way, and in fact the author of Chronicles dates the beginning of the reform six years earlier than the finding of the book (2 Chr. 34: 3–7). The book in question was certainly Deuteronomy, or so the author wished it to be understood. But whether the account of its discovery is historical and, if so, whether it really had been lost or whether it was 'planted' by the reform party for their own purposes, no doubt with the best of intentions, are questions which can no longer be answered with certainty. The fact that the account of the discovery of the book in the temple is part of the so-called Deuteronomistic History, from the same 'school' as Deuteronomy, also suggests the possibility that it is a fiction designed to explain how the law could have been neglected to such a scandalous extent during the long reign of Manasseh, grandfather of Josiah.

The movement of religious renewal which gathered strength during Josiah's reign coincided with Judah's bid for independence from the Assyrians after more than a century of vassalage. This attempt would have had a chance of success only after the death of Ashurbanipal, the last effective king of Assyria, in 627 BCE, and it is not without significance that the Chronicler dates the religious reforms to within a year of that time. Bids for independence from imperial control generally went in tandem with a revival of national cults, and the coincidence will help to explain the warlike tone and strong nationalist sentiment apparent throughout Deuteronomy.

Religious reform had been going on intermittently throughout the history of Judah almost from the beginning, which of course means that none of these reforms, including those of Josiah, had any lasting success. The most vigorous effort was made during the reign of Hezekiah (c.715–687 BCE) whose concern was that Judah should not share the fate of the Kingdom of Samaria recently incorporated into the Assyrian empire. Here, too, cultic reform went hand in hand with an attempt at political emancipation from the Assyrian overlord and included the important innovation of attempting to abolish the high places (2 Kgs. 18: 3–8, 22); in which respect Hezekiah anticipated the aims of the reform party during Josiah's reign. There is a certain convergence of indications that a great deal of writing was going on during the reign of Hezekiah, the first monarch to rule in Judah without a counterpart in the kingdom to the north. Biblical tradition attributes the composition of a psalm to him (Isa. 38: 9), the collecting, copying, and editing of proverbs is ascribed to 'Hezekiah's men' (Prov. 25: 1), the contemporary prophet Isaiah exhibits a high level of literary ability, and the greatest concentration of inscribed material dates from this time (e.g. ostraca from several sites including Arad and Jerusalem, seals and stamped jar handles, and the famous Siloam inscription). In view of the scribal character of Deuteronomy, and its high esteem for law as the peculiarly Israelite embodiment of wisdom (e.g. Deut. 4: 5–8), it is quite possible that the book began to take shape at that time. We conclude, then, that Deuteronomy was the literary production of scribal circles attached to the Judean court, that it matured over a considerable period of time as the programme of a reforming, nationalistic party, and that it was meant to serve as a blueprint for a constitution embodying the agenda of that party.

In describing Josiah's reforms, the historian speaks only of affirming Yahwistic orthodoxy and rejecting pagan or syncretist practices. Neither here, nor anywhere else in the history of reform, is there the slightest allusion to the removal of such social abuses as were condemned by the prophets. The Deuteronomic law, on the other hand, juxtaposes fidelity to the cult of Yahweh with the task of creating a just society. Its utopian character is apparent in its abolition of poverty—'there will be no poor among you' (15: 4)—and its overriding insistence on justice in every aspect of national life—'justice, and only justice, you shall pursue' (16: 20). But it also legislated in favour of the disadvantaged classes of society including widows, orphans, resident aliens, and the unemployed. It goes beyond the Covenant Code in its insistence on the remission of debts in the seventh year and adds appropriate measures to prevent evasion or abuse of the law (15: 1–11). Usury and abusive debt collection, which had contributed to driving many farmers off the land, are prohibited (23: 19–20; 24: 6, 10–13, 17), and there are provisions for the protection and, in some cases, the emancipation of slaves which go beyond measures in the Covenant Code (15: 12–18; 23: 15–16; 24: 7).

The Deuteronomic legislation reflects awareness of the fact that measures of this kind, however well-intentioned, are not likely to be effective so long as the institutional structures of the society remain immune to reform and regeneration. There are therefore stipulations concerning the conduct of local judges (16: 18–20), to which is added the innovation of a central judiciary and court of appeals referred to earlier (17: 8–13). There are also provisions governing the employment and support of clergy (18: 1–8) and, most significantly, a 'mirror for kings' which, in effect, sets up a constitutional monarchy (17: 14–20).

Several of the Deuteronomic laws are designed to protect individual rights, including those of the free farmer. One example is the ancient prohibition against removing boundary marks (19: 14), which occurs also in the instructions (e.g. Prov. 22: 28). Concern for property, one's own and that of others, is evident throughout, and even extends to birds' nests (22: 6–7). The priestly tithe is quite restricted (18: 1–8), and support of the national cult, another problem area, is to be proportionate to the individual's means (16: 6–7). However, such measures do not disguise the fact that the Deuteronomic law is, first and foremost, a state document, a constitution, or at least a blueprint for a constitution. As such, it necessarily aimed to undermine the traditional, regional social structures based on kinship, real or fictitious. We note, without going into great detail, how state-appointed judges (16: 18–20; 17: 8–13) were taking over the functions of the elders and the local head of household (e.g. 19: 15–21; 21: 1–9; 25: 1–3). The law of sanctuary greatly restricted the age-old practice of the blood feud (19: 1–13), and several judicial operations were removed from the jurisdiction of the head of household (e.g. 21: 15–17, 18–21). The requirement that adult males present themselves three times a year at the central sanctuary (16: 16) aimed at transferring loyalty from the local kinship group, the clan, and its annual gathering and sacrifice (e.g. 1 Sam. 20: 5–6, 28–9) to the state cult; prohibitions against death rituals and mortuary practices (14: 1; 18: 9–14; 26: 14) took aim at the cult of ancestors, an essential aspect of the kinship ethos; and the cultic centralization programme announced at the beginning of the law (ch. 12) served the purpose of imposing both religious and political unity.

A vigorous debate which has been going on among Old Testament scholars for almost two centuries has to do with the authorship of the Deuteronomic programme. The high level of interest in this issue is understandable, since we are dealing with a text which marks the watershed between Israel as a nation state and Judaism as a religion based on law and worship. At one time it seemed well established that its origins were to be sought in the territory of the Northern Kingdom. Similarities with the so-called Elohist source in the Pentateuch (E), allegedly of northern provenance, and with the Ephraimite prophet Hosea, were adduced in evidence. The Elohist narrative strand has, however, proved to be elusive, and its northern origin difficult to establish with a comfortable degree of probability. Deuteronomy certainly reflects the language of Hosea at several points, but it also owes a debt to Judaean prophets. Hosea, moreover, shows practically no concern with the kind of social abuses which Deuteronomy combats.

Another line of enquiry traces the distinctive character of the book, and especially its strong homiletic style, to Levites, again with special emphasis on northern Levites. On this point we have a terminological problem. As a class of second-order clergy, assistants to the sacrificing priesthood, Levites are not unambiguously attested in pre-exilic texts. Deuteronomy itself refers to Levites as a distinct and subordinate clerical class only in one passage (27: 14) which belongs to the latest editorial stratum of the book. The 'levitical priests' referred to throughout Deuteronomy are not of this kind. The term seems to have been adopted, doubtless for polemical reasons, to signify that these constitute the traditional and therefore legitimate priestly class, as opposed to the non-levitical priesthood installed in the Northern Kingdom by Jeroboam (1 Kgs. 12: 31), and perhaps also the Aaronite faction which had not yet achieved supremacy (Deut. 9: 20). Sympathy for the 'levitical' priesthood, in evidence throughout the book, suggests that its authors belonged to a scribal class of literati and legal experts closely allied to the priesthood, one which perhaps came into existence as a state-appointed scribal specialization of the priestly office.

We can summarize this part of our discussion as follows. The Deuteronomic programme represents a deposit of religious and social reform which peaked shortly after the destruction of the Northern Kingdom (722 BCE), was dormant during the long reign of Manasseh (687–642 BCE), and achieved its greatest, if no less short-lived, success under Josiah (640–609 BCE). An important factor in this sporadic movement of reform was prophetic preaching, and here the operative distinction is not so much between northern and southern prophets as between provincial and metropolitan. Micah came not from Jerusalem but from a town called Moresheth in the Judaean foothills south-west of the capital. We know that he influenced the reforms of Hezekiah (see Jer. 26: 16–19), and there are numerous points of contact between his indictment of his contemporaries and the social legislation in Deuteronomy, e.g. removing landmarks, usury, unjust exploitation of debtors, falsifying weights and measures, and bribery. This leads us to suspect that the initial impetus to reform, generated by Micah and perhaps other prophets like him, came from outside Jerusalem, perhaps via the social class referred to as 'the people of the land'. It was this class which put Josiah on the throne (2 Kgs. 21: 24), and therefore was presumably in a position to promote its own agenda. It seems to have retained its political influence down to the end of national independence (e.g. 2 Kgs. 25: 15).

But there is another side to Deuteronomy, one of particular interest for our theme, namely, its scribal character and its character as a state document. This aspect is apparent in the insistence that the laws be studied, explained, and taught (e.g. 1: 5; 4: 1, 10, 36; 5: 1) as a God-given discipline (4: 36; 8: 5; 11: 2), and that their study and observance is the way to wisdom (4: 6). Moses is presented as teacher and scribe; as such, he not only enunciates the laws but provides motivation for their observance, e.g. in the refrain that runs through the book, 'that you may live long in the land which Yahweh your God is giving you'. Exhortations to take heed, to recall the experiences of the past, to acknowledge the truth of what is being said, give a character and tone to the book which inevitably call to mind the style of the sages in Proverbs and other sapiential compositions. There can be no doubt, therefore, that in Deuteronomy the legal and sapiential traditions flow together.

One effect of the confluence of the two traditions, the legal and the sapiential–didactic, is to modify the sense of the law as a purely objective and extrinsic reality. The presentation of the legal compilations under the broader category of instruction mitigates the sense of law as bald, divine command hedging in the autonomy of the individual addressed. The 'sapientializing' of the law suggests that it is to be internalized by an activity which unites learning and piety in the pursuit of a goal freely chosen:

You will seek Yahweh your God, and you will find him if you search after him with all your heart and soul.   (4: 29)

It is this *searching*, through study and observance of Torah, which will emerge with increasing clarity as the hallmark of early Judaism after the return from the exile.

It was suggested earlier that this scribal character of the book resulted from its character as an official state document. The royal scribe, attested from the time of the United Monarchy, was a high official with a wide range of responsibilities. During the reign of Josiah the royal scribe Shaphan supervised the repair of the temple and it was to him that the scroll found there was handed. It was also he who read it to the king and who was sent to consult with the prophetess Huldah as to what should be done about it (2 Kgs. 22: 3–20). This does not, of course, imply that he and his colleagues at the court were responsible for writing the book, as some have suggested. It seems much more likely that it was redacted by law scribes or 'handlers of the law' (Jer. 2: 8) who formed a specialized corps within the ranks of the temple clergy and were the ancestors of the levitical scribes of the Second Temple period. We have seen that this was a new development, since specialized legal interpretation was called for only when there was an authoritative written law to be interpreted. Its importance for the future can hardly be exaggerated.

If this is so, it would follow that the same class was responsible for the mature formulations of ideas about the covenant which we find in Deuteronomy. It is at this point that the political analogy, i.e., appeal to Assyrian vassal treaties, carries most weight. The book itself testifies to its character as a political manifesto, a declaration of independence from foreign control and a reaffirmation of national identity. While repudiating links with foreign 'principalities and powers', Deuteronomy reaffirms Israel's covenant bond with Yahweh as the source of its collective existence. The strength of this reaffirmation was such that, even though the bid for independence and the religious reforms themselves were short-lived, it could still provide inspiration for the new generation which returned to the land after the exile.

5

Law in Early Judaism: Temple Community and Sect

The Priestly History

The Pentateuch was created by a decision to conclude the history of founding events with the death of Moses. As to when, and under what circumstances, this decision was taken, we are for the most part in the dark. It certainly corresponds to the great importance assigned to law as the foundation of the social life of the restored community after the return from exile, and to Moses as the mediator of this divinely revealed law. It could also have been due, in part, to political pressures exerted on the province of Judah by the Persian imperial administration. At the most obvious level, an account of the conquest of Palestine with fire and sword would not have been greeted with enthusiasm by Persian officials. But we also know that it was Persian policy to insist on the compilation, promulgation, and observance of local, traditional laws, including laws governing worship, in the provinces of their vast empire. As early as the reign of Cyrus, we hear complaints of royal commissioners that Babylonian priests were negligent in carrying out the cult of Marduk, the local deity. Somewhat later, Darius commissioned a codification of traditional Egyptian laws and, later still, a letter written by the satrap of Egypt ordered the Jewish military colony at Elephantine on the Upper Nile to celebrate the feast of Unleavened Bread in the proper, traditional manner. Another Persian king sent Ezra as a kind of royal commissioner to Jerusalem to see that the 'law of the God of heaven' was known and enforced among Jews in the Trans-Euphrates satrapy (Ezra 7: 11–26). The final compilation and redaction of the laws may therefore have been mandated by the authorities as the civil and religious constitution of the province of Yehud (Judah), or even of the Jewish ethnos throughout the Iranian empire.

Let us add that, since the custom of presenting laws in a narrative context was already well established by that time, the consolidation of the legal heritage would have implied a comparable reshaping of the story of founding events.

In order to grasp the point and purpose of the cultic and ritual laws, we must begin with the narrative context in which they are presented. If we ignore, for the moment, the cut-off point at the death of Moses (Deut. 34), we have a continuous narrative from Creation to the Babylonian exile, corresponding to the first nine books of the Bible (Genesis, Exodus, Leviticus, Numbers, Deuteronomy, Joshua, Judges, Samuel, Kings). In the previous chapter we saw that Deuteronomy is a distinct composition and is closely related, perhaps as a kind of theological preface, to the Deuteronomistic History (hereafter Dtr.) from Joshua to Kings. The connection need not be argued in detail; the reader may simply note that rulers are evaluated according to their observance or non-observance of the Deuteronomic law, and prophets fill the role assigned to them in Deut. 18: 15–22.

The first four books of the Pentateuch, which tell the story from Creation to the end of Israel's wandering in the wilderness, present problems of a more formidable nature, several of them still without a solution. Our concern is with the legal material in these books, but the point has been made more than once that the laws can be understood only in the narrative context in which they are presented. This context must therefore first be discussed, if only in a brief and summary fashion. Beginning with the Creation account in Gen. 1: 1–2: 4, a narrative line with its own highly characteristic terminology and themes serves as the context for a great mass of cultic and ritual legislation. This Priestly narrative and law (designated P) alternates with narrative of a quite different kind. On this alternative narrative, the classical documentary hypothesis held that it was composed of two strands, running more or less parallel and based on a common stock of traditional material, which strands were transmitted separately in the Northern and Southern kingdoms. At some point, shortly before or after the fall of the Northern Kingdom in the late eighth century BCE, they were conflated in Judah, resulting in one epic narrative of the nation's origins. This appears to have been a time of intense literary activity both in Israel and in neighbouring lands. The Assyrian kings, for example, were at that time assembling and editing ancient mythological and epic texts for their great library in Nineveh and, further afield, the Homeric poems were being written up in their present form.

While there are many scholars who would still accept an explanation more or less along these lines, there are others who question the extent, date, or even existence of such early sources, and it would be safe to say there is no longer a consensus. For our purpose it will be unnecessary to argue the case further. It will suffice to make the point that, since the principal theme of the story of Israel's ancestors in Genesis 12–50 is the promise of nationhood and land, this basic narrative must have included the occupation of Canaan and therefore have constituted a Hexateuch rather than a Pentateuch (i.e., a six-book collection including Joshua).

To return to the Priestly History: with its highly distinctive style, fondness for genealogies and concern for exact chronology, P has proved to be the easiest of the narrative strands in the Pentateuch to identify. One problem, however, concerns its extent. All agree that it opens with the Creation recital in Genesis 1: 1—2: 4, which highlights the seven-day liturgical week, the fixing of the religious calendar (on the fourth day, 1: 14), and sabbath (2: 2–3), but there is no firm consensus as to its ending. Some scholars bring it to an end with the death of Moses, described in typically Priestly language at the end of Deuteronomy:

Then Moses went up from the plains of Moab to Mount Nebo . . . which is opposite Jericho . . . Moses was one hundred and twenty years old when he died; his sight was unimpaired, and his vigor was unabated. The Israelites wept for Moses in the plains of Moab thirty days; then the period of mourning for Moses was ended. Joshua son of Nun was full of the spirit of wisdom, because Moses had laid his hands on him; and the Israelites obeyed him, doing as Yahweh had commanded Moses. (34: 1, 7–9)

The more probable alternative, however, is that it continues on to the setting up of the wilderness sanctuary in Canaan and the partitioning of the land among the tribes towards the end of Joshua:

Then the whole congregation of the Israelites assembled at Shiloh, and set up the tent of meeting there. The land lay subdued before them . . . These are the inheritances that the priest Eleazar and Joshua son of Nun and the heads of the families of the tribes of the Israelites distributed by lot at Shiloh before Yahweh, at the entrance of the tent of meeting. So they finished dividing the land. (Josh. 18: 1; 19: 51)

The technical vocabulary in this passage is Priestly, the partitioning of the land under civil and religious leadership is in accord with the situation at the time of the Second Commonwealth and, most significantly, the episode fits the structure of the P history as a whole. That structure pivots on the creation of the world as a cosmic sanctuary for worshipping God (Gen. 1: 1—2: 4), the setting up of the sanctuary and inauguration of worship in the wilderness of Sinai (Exod. 25–31; 35–40), and the final coming to rest of the same sanctuary in the Promised Land (Josh. 18–19). The structure encodes an interpretation of the history as the progressive revelation of a cultic order by means of which God has chosen to be present to his people. In keeping with this perspective, the Priestly version of the promise of land and nationhood is amplified with the promise of divine presence effected through worship: 'I will be your God, I will be with you'.

Another aspect of the Priestly History currently being debated is its relation to the non-Priestly material in the Pentateuch. Some scholars regard P as an editorial strand which is meant to be read together with the (presumed older) narrative sources, while others read it as an independent and self-standing narrative. It is easy to overlook that the issue cannot be decided apart from the question of the final editing of the Pentateuch or Hexateuch; for if P is not identical with this final redaction, as seems entirely possible, the selection and combination of Priestly and non-Priestly narrative could have left *both* incomplete when taken by themselves. Structurally, at any rate, the core P narrative gives every sign of being a well-thought-out and crafted story, as we have seen.

We now return to the further and final stage by which we arrive at a Pentateuch rather than a Hexateuch, a stage which is without doubt the most neglected in critical study to date. All we can do here is present a possible reconstruction in the barest outline. At some point Deuteronomy was incorporated into the basic narrative of the

Priestly school. When this happened, or perhaps at some later point, the decision was also made to bring the story to an end with the death of Moses, thus excluding the account of the conquest and settlement. According to the mainline P narrative Moses is commanded in the wilderness to commission Joshua as his successor, go up Mount Abarim, and die, and the implication clearly is that this is to happen at once (Num. 27: 12–23), as it happened with Miriam (Num. 20: 1) and, at greater length, with Aaron (Num. 20: 22–9). But Moses does not die at once, and the reason is that once Deuteronomy was incorporated into the history, the death of Moses had to be postponed to allow him to present a new covenant and law in Moab. The Priestly editor who made these adjustments simply added a date in the P style at the beginning of Deuteronomy (1: 3), thus bringing the entire book elegantly within the P chronology, and introduced an updated version of the commissioning of Joshua, concluding with the death of Moses at the end (Deut. 32: 48–52; 34: 1, 7–9).

The general reader may be excused for being impatient with these hypothetical reconstructions, but the fact of the matter is that the stages by which the Pentateuch reached its present form correspond to different stages in the religious history of Israel and early Judaism. And, apropos of our theme, it is possible to understand the development of the legal tradition only in the context of this literary history. A people retains its vitality, even its identity, only at the price of continually rethinking and reappropriating its traditions in the light of new situations, especially when these situations are of a profoundly disorientating kind. That Torah was brought to an end with the death of Moses rather than with the conquest of the land, for example, corresponds to a very significant shift in the way post-exilic Judaism came to understand its own character and destiny. At an earlier stage, the different ways in which the Priestly source (P) edited or amplified the existing narrative traditions provide important clues to the adjustments and changes forced on the community as a result of political disaster and exile.

Some of the more prominent characteristics of the P history relevant to an understanding of the legislation are the following:

1. The addiction of P to genealogies can be explained by the need for continuity after the political disasters of the fall of Jerusalem and

exile, linked with the need for legitimation with the emergence of a new order. We see from the long list of Babylonian immigrants in Ezra 2 (= Nehemiah 7) that one's civic status depended on proving one's descent. The genealogy which interrupts the P version of Moses' commissioning (Exod. 6: 14–25), for example, traces the priestly lineage back to Aaron, elder brother of Moses, and through him to Levi, and thus established the temple priesthood of the early post-exilic period on a firm basis of antiquity.

2. The greatly enhanced role of Aaron in the same P version of the commissioning of Moses (Exod. 6: 2—7: 7, cf. the earlier version, 3: 1—6: 1) reflects the dominant position won by this branch of the priesthood after the return from exile and re-establishment of worship in Jerusalem. In the temple-community established at that time the priesthood took over some of the functions of the monarchy after the latter had disappeared from history. It also helped that the Persian authorities tended to favour priesthoods as instruments of the *pax Persica* in the provinces.

3. The need to guard against the dangers of assimilation, a major preoccupation during the exile and after the return to the land, is reflected in the P version of the Jacob saga. It is the Priestly editor who explains Jacob's flight to Mesopotamia by the need to avoid marriage with a Canaanite woman, and holds up Esau's marriage with Hittite women as an example of the deplorable effects of such unions (Gen. 26: 34–5; 27: 46—28: 5). P is, nevertheless, remarkably universalistic in outlook. All humanity receives a religious qualification at Creation, the first covenant is made with the new humanity to preserve the restored but damaged world after the deluge, the same humanity receives the first law for its guidance (the so-called Noachide law, Gen. 9: 1–7), and at numerous points the P legislation insists that the native-born and resident alien receive the same treatment. This universalism contrasts notably with the nationalistic spirit and ethos of Deuteronomy.

4. The P narrative modifies the standard, Deuteronomic understanding of covenant. Only in P does God make a covenant with Noah, and therefore with humanity, in the archaic period before Israel came into existence (Gen. 9: 8–17). The covenant with the ancestors (Gen. 17: 1–21) is the only covenant God makes with Israel. Both are described as 'perpetual' (Gen. 9: 16; 17: 7, 13),

meaning that, unlike political covenants, they do not require periodic renewal and revalidation. All that is required is that God *remember* his covenant, which he does when his people call on him (Exod. 2: 24; Lev. 26: 42, 45). The P version of the Sinai story, therefore, has no covenant other than the observance of sabbath, described also as perpetual (Exod. 31: 12–17). The Priestly covenant is also distinctive in that it is no longer genuinely bilateral. In other words, and unlike the Deuteronomic pattern, God's commitment made in the covenant is not contingent on the fulfilment of certain conditions, or on a certain level of moral performance, by Israel or humanity.

It was along these lines, then, that the history was reinterpreted by the Priestly school to meet the critical situation following the disasters of the sixth century BCE and, at the same time, maintain essential links with the past. With the gradual return to the homeland after the Persian conquest of Babylon (539 BCE), Judah took shape as one of several provinces in one of the twenty satrapies of the Persian empire. Like some of the Greek city-states in Ionia, its status was determined by its temple which served not only as a place of prayer and sacrifice but as a major administrative and financial centre of the province. The civic status of the individual, even perhaps title to property, depended on participation in and support of temple worship. Hence the great power of the priesthood in both the religious and political sphere, backed as it was by the central government which subsidized the cult (cf. Ezra 6: 4, 8). This was the social situation in which, in all probability, the P cultic and ritual laws were compiled.

Cultic and ritual laws

In many traditional societies, Israel included, correct cultic performance was an essential aspect of public order and well-being. To participate in public worship in Israel was a way of sharing in the praise and adoration of God carried on unceasingly in the heavenly world. By doing so, one fulfilled the goal of existence. Recall how Isaiah received his prophetic commission through a vision in which he was admitted to this heavenly liturgy and heard the seraphim singing the divine praise (Isa. 6: 1–13). The same idea appears here and there in the Psalms, and when God answered Job out of the whirlwind he spoke of the dedication liturgy accompanying the laying of the foundation stone of the vast temple of the world:

> Where were you when I laid the foundation of the earth?
>   Tell me, if you have understanding.
> Who determined its measurements—surely you know!
>   Or who stretched the line upon it?
> On what were its bases sunk,
>   or who laid its cornerstone,
> when the morning stars sang together,
>   and all the heavenly beings shouted for joy? (Job 38: 4–7)

The importance of the liturgical calendar, as marking the course of sacred time, is indicated by its origins in the first week of Creation (Gen. 1: 14). Similar considerations operated on the spatial axis, since the sanctuary was constructed according to a heavenly blueprint received by Moses from God in a vision (Exod. 25: 9, 40; 26: 30). To share in worship then, was to participate to the fullest extent in reality and to live according to a divinely willed order.

It follows, according to this world-view, that the purpose of the many cultic acts carried out in the temple was to maintain and, where necessary, restore this divine order. Sin, even inadvertent sin, was understood as a disturbance of that order. The sacrificial cult was in fact designed primarily, if not exclusively, to remove the effects of inadvertent sin. Though the situation is not entirely clear, it seems that for deliberate sinful acts, those committed 'with a high hand' (Num. 15: 30–1), remission through the cult was not possible. In rejecting the law, the sinner rejected its author, thereby putting himself outside the community and beyond the reach of the redemptive possibilities available within it.

Part of our problem in understanding, let alone accepting, such a way of thinking, can perhaps be dissolved at the linguistic level. These Judean priests clearly had a broader concept of sin than is common among religious people today. For them 'sin' meant 'disorder', and disorder could come about by human activity which we would not regard as sinful. To be in a sinful state is therefore not just a matter of ethics as we understand it. It is to be, for whatever reason, in a wrong relationship to an order which is built into the fabric of a world created by God. Hence the concern in the ritual law for bodily states, the integrity of the body, the protection of its orifices as its boundaries with the rest of the world, the food we ingest, physical contacts, and the like. By the same token, holiness is not just a matter of internal states and acts. It must also encompass the material world, and therefore also the body as that part of the world for which each one is more directly responsible.

Before going any further, a word should be said about dating the P material. The majority opinion today is that the vast complex of Priestly narrative and law comes from the period of the ascendancy of the Aaronite priesthood, that is, from no earlier than the first phase of the Babylonian exile (587/6–538 BCE). This opinion does not, of course, exclude the possibility that cultic and ritual data of much greater antiquity have been incorporated into the P complex, especially since cultic and ritual language tends to be very conservative. A minority opinion builds on the arguments of the Israeli scholar Yehezkel Kaufmann who opted for a date several centuries earlier, partly on linguistic grounds, partly in opposition to the ideologically motivated late dating of P by Wellhausen and other scholars unsympathetic to the priesthood and to Judaism *tout court*. The matter cannot be discussed at the level of detail it deserves, but the following brief observations are in order. Arguments from linguistic usage (paired words for the same item, one early, one later; one word used with two different meanings, one early, one later) are weak, both because of the conservative nature of cultic language and the cult's addiction to archaism, and also because the absence of fixed chronological points of reference in biblical texts leads to circular argumentation. It must also be borne in mind that P is a complex, multi-generational literary product, with regard to both narrative and law. We have tried to show that the core P narrative is carefully structured and that it best fits the situation immediately preceding or at some point after the resumption of temple worship in the Persian province of Judah. Since the narrative provides the context for the cultic and ritual legislation, we conclude that the latter was very probably compiled at the same time, with older material incorporated and much supplementary material added even later.

The history as narrated by P serves primarily to display the orderly revelation of those cultic institutions on which the welfare of the community depends. The succession of events leads up to the climactic moment of Sinai when, and only when, sacrifice could be offered after the ordination of Aaron and his sons. Unlike the alternative narrative, therefore, P will not allow Noah to sacrifice after leaving the ark, or the ancestors to do so on their wanderings through Canaan. In the pre-Sinaitic period only those institutions are established which do not call for the presence of a priest—the prohibition of eating bloody meat, encumbent on all (Gen. 9: 4–6), then, for Israel, circumcision (Gen. 17: 9–14), Passover (Exod. 12: 1–20), and sabbath (Ex.31: 12–17), the celebration of which was adumbrated in Creation and anticipated in the wilderness (Exod. 16: 5, 22–30).

The bulk of the cultic and ritual law is in Leviticus and Numbers, and is presented as given by Yahweh from the sanctuary immediately after its construction at Sinai. P notes carefully the exact time of Israel's arrival at and departure from Sinai (Exod. 19: 1; Num. 10: 11–28). According to P the Sinai event consists not in the making of a covenant but in the establishment of the cult. Moses encounters the mysterious presence of God, the divine 'glory', on the mountain, is given the detailed specifications for the wilderness sanctuary and its appointments (25–31), and sees to their execution (35–40). As noted a moment ago, the only legal enactment mentioned here is the sabbath rest, enjoined under pain of death. It is to be a sign of Creation and, like circumcision, a perpetual covenant (Exod. 31: 12–17).

Leviticus, known in Jewish tradition as 'the law of the priests', contains several collections of cultic and ritual law which were originally distinct. Leviticus 1–7, one of these, is a small manual specifying the different kinds of sacrifice and the economically important matter of allocating sacrificial material. That it was an originally independent booklet is apparent from the fact that Leviticus 8–10 continues the Priestly Sinai narrative. These chapters treat of the ordination of Aaron and his sons as priests, the inauguration of their priesthood, and the elimination of the two elder sons, Nadab and Abihu, for failure to observe the exact ritual. This last episode, incidentally, is one of several in P which reflect the struggle for power among priestly families, resulting in one branch firmly in control. Another collection, Leviticus 11–15, deals with ritual impurity and bodily emissions. It is followed by the ritual for the Day of Atonement (Yom Kippur) in Leviticus 16 which may be of quite late date since the great fast and penitential rite invoked by Ezra followed different rules (Neh. 9: 1). The most important collection, however, is the one known to modern scholarship as the Holiness Code (H), widely thought to be a separate text covering various aspects of the demand for holiness (Lev. 17–26).

A glance at the contents of Leviticus 17–26 will show that it is by no means as orderly or homogeneous as the title 'Holiness Code' might lead one to think. Like the Deuteronomic law, it opens with a prohibition of eating meat with the blood in it. In both cases reasons are given for the prohibition (Lev. 17). The next chapter (Lev. 18) gives the impression of being a separate manual containing a series of twelve types of forbidden sexual relations. These are followed by other offences which defile the land: sexual relations with a woman during her period, adultery, the sacrifice of children (the so-called *molech* sacrifices attested among the Phoenicians and Carthaginians), homosexuality and bestiality. The section begins and ends with divine address presenting these laws as safeguarding the life and character of Israel as it prepares to live in its own land.

So far there has been no mention of holiness. The demand that the people be holy in conformity with the holiness of their God occurs for the first time at the beginning and end of the next section (Lev. 19–20):

You shall be holy; for I, Yahweh your God, am holy. (19: 2)

I am Yahweh your God; I have separated you from the peoples. You shall therefore make a distinction between the clean animal and the unclean, and between the unclean bird and the clean . . . You shall be holy to me; for I Yahweh am holy, and I have separated you from the other peoples to be mine. (20: 24–6)

The stipulations in this section are both ethical and ritual, though this distinction would not have been as obvious to the redactors of the laws and those to whom they were addressed as it is to us. Leaving aside Leviticus 19: 5–9, which is an appendix to the rules governing sacrifice in Leviticus 3, we find here most of the stipulations of the Decalogue together with laws against necromancy (black magic) and a variety of pagan practices, some of them associated with the cult of the dead. Somewhat surprisingly, however, these are juxtaposed with dispositions in favour of the poor and disadvantaged in society, e.g. gleaning rights, the prompt payment of wages, and care for the deaf, blind, and aged.

As in the Deuteronomic legislation, with which this section has much in common, one has the impression that these measures are only examples of what is involved in creating and maintaining a just and orderly society. They are summarized in the command to love and not to hate:

You shall not hate in your heart any one of your kin; you shall reprove your neighbour, or you will incur guilt yourself. You shall not take vengeance or bear a grudge against any of your people, but you shall love your neighbour as yourself: I am Yahweh. (19: 17–18)

While, in the context, 'neighbour' means fellow-Jew, it should be noted that the obligation also covers resident aliens:

When an alien resides with you in your land, you shall not oppress an alien. The alien who resides with you shall be to you as the citizen among you; you shall love the alien as yourself, for you were aliens in the land of Egypt: I am Yahweh your God. (19: 33–4)

Following prophetic precedent, Jesus coupled this command with the Shema ('Hear, O Israel'; Deut. 6: 4–9) as a summary of the entire Torah (Matt. 22: 34–40).

The last part of this section (Lev. 20) contains, for the most part, the penalties attached to violations of the 'sexual dodecalogue'; i.e., the twelve-unit series in Leviticus 18. Its conclusion, quoted above, suggests that Leviticus 19–20 is a self-contained unit which could more properly be called the Holiness Code than the larger composition to which that title is generally applied. The following chapters contain rules more specifically addressed to the priesthood (Lev. 21–2), a liturgical calendar (Lev. 23), and various stipulations concerning worship, the sabbatical year and the jubilee year (Lev. 24–5). As in Deuteronomy, the laws are rounded off with blessings and curses. These clearly reflect the exilic situation when Israel's God will remember his covenant with the ancestors (26: 40–2). It is also stated that the God whose will finds expression in the laws is also the God who sets free:

I am Yahweh your God who brought you out of the land of Egypt, to be their slaves no more; I have broken the bars of your yoke and made you walk erect. (26: 13)

In Leviticus and Numbers the ideal of holiness comes to expression in these and similar laws and, more generally, in the description of Israel in its wanderings through the desert to the promised land. Given the assumptions on which secular life is based, it is not easy for us today to grasp what holiness meant to the authors of these texts. It is clearly not restricted to the moral life as this is generally understood. Rather than imitating God ethically, whatever that might mean, to strive for holiness like the holiness of God meant to orient one's life according to what was revealed about the character and activity of God. Translated into principles of conduct, this imitation of God implied not only a high ethical ideal but a distinctive way of life which set the community apart from surrounding cultures. Whatever the remote origin of rules governing food taboos and ritual defilement, which are not confined to ancient Israel and Judaism, it is more important to understand how they functioned as means of defining and maintaining this distinctive character.

To take only one example: the vigilance concerning the exercise of the sexual function, apparent in the Holiness Code, has to be seen as a reaction to the sacralization of sexuality in Canaanite fertility cults, with their 'holy ones' (cultic prostitutes, male and female) and orgiastic rites. During and after the exile, the purity laws acted as a counter to the endemic tendency towards assimilation. With the growth of the diaspora, demographic expansion, and the adherence of increasing numbers of Gentiles to the Jewish faith, this tendency was bound to get stronger. On the other hand, it was also inevitable that, as Judaism became a world-wide faith, criticism would be increasingly levelled at these highly distinctive features which by then had achieved confessional status. This, however, belongs to a later stage of the history.

The world inhabited by Israel's priests seems far distant from that of the sages. Yet in some ways the literary productions of the priesthood we have been considering, often maligned in modern Christian scholarship, attest to a more developed if more idiosyncratic intellectualism than the so-called 'wisdom writings'. These priests did not elaborate a theory of ritual, they were not anthropologists, but it can be shown (and has been shown) that the ritual laws of clean and unclean cohere in a taxonomic system, a sociocultural code by means of which the individual could locate himself or herself within an orderly cosmos and society.

Add that the roles priests were called on to fill called for a wide range of knowledge, legal, medical, astronomical, and ritual. The acquisition of this knowledge and the practical skills associated with it required training, on which unfortunately we have little or no information. There must have been an educational institution of some kind associated with the Jerusalem temple, comparable to the Egyptian 'house of life' mentioned earlier, and such training centres must have existed among the diaspora communities in Southern Mesopotamia. We learn that, before setting out on his mission, Ezra recruited temple personnel from 'the place Casiphia', presumably a cult establishment or clergy training centre of some kind (Ezra 8: 15–20). Priests also served as teachers, legal experts, and magistrates, though in the course of time these activities tended to be taken over by Levites and, eventually, by lay specialists.

Wisdom and law in the Chronicler's work

Historiography was not generally considered an important form of intellectual activity in antiquity. In fifth-century BCE Greece, Herodotus and his Ionian predecessors were followed by Thucydides, but they had no imitators. For the first history of Babylon and Egypt we have to wait until the Hellenistic period when Berossus wrote his *Babyloniaka* and Manetho his *Aegyptiaka*. Before that time we have nothing more substantial in length and scope than commemorative records of military campaigns, construction and dedication of temples, and the like. In Israel (Judah), by the fifth century BCE, two substantial historical works were in existence, the Dtr. and the P History. How much of historical interest was written during the monarchy we do not know. Records would have been kept in the royal palace and temple in Jerusalem, both torched by the Babylonian commander Nebuzaradan. Works of any length would, moreover, have been written on papyrus, a writing surface particularly vulnerable to the Palestinian climate. A first edition of Dtr., composed during Josiah's reign, may have survived, but we are in the dark as to whether anything else of a historical nature was written under the monarchy.

The Hebrew Bible has preserved another large-scale historical work: 1 and 2 Chronicles with Ezra and Nehemiah which, taken together, cover a vast sweep from Creation to the mission of Nehemiah in the fifth century BCE. This work draws on both earlier histories by using the Priestly genealogies to bridge the gap between Creation and the monarchy (1 Chr. 1–9) and Dtr. from the death of Saul to the Babylonian exile. Its relationship to these earlier works is not entirely clear. It may have been intended to supplant them but, if so, it appears that they were too firmly established for this to be possible. Another debated issue is the process by which the Chronicler's history reached its final form. That there were earlier drafts seems well established. That it drew on a somewhat different version of the history from the one now contained in the books of Samuel and Kings is at least possible. Some have found confirmation for this hypothesis in certain manuscript fragments of Samuel discovered in the fourth Qumran cave which are closer to Chronicles than to our Hebrew text of Samuel. For our present purpose this particular issue need not be pursued further.

Whatever its previous stages, the final version cannot be dated earlier than the last events recorded in it, and these take us to the late fifth or early fourth century BCE. (We assume that 1–2 Chronicles–Ezra–Nehemiah is meant to be read as a single work, as the repetition of the final paragraph of 2 Chronicles at the beginning of Ezra suggests). The absence of any allusion to the end of Persian rule, and the author's sympathetic attitude to Persian rulers, suggest a date prior to the conquest of Alexander in 332 BCE. But this is only an educated guess, and would not in any case preclude later additions, e.g. some of the genealogies and the Memoir of Nehemiah.

To come to the point which concerns us in this chapter, the Chronicler gives pride of place to 'the law of Moses' which he takes to be a law available in writing from the beginning. The frequent allusions which he makes to this law do not, however, necessarily point to the Pentateuch as we have it today in its final form. In dealing with legal matters he refers sometimes to Deuteronomy, sometimes to ritual laws in Leviticus and Numbers, and sometimes to enactments which either differ in some respect from Pentateuchal law or are not in the Pentateuch at all.

At one point he presents what purports to be a letter from the Persian king Artaxerxes—the context would naturally suggest Artaxerxes I (464–425 BCE)—authorizing Ezra, a priest and scribe, to see that 'the law of the God of heaven' was known, understood, and observed among the Jews living in the Trans-Euphrates satrapy of the Persian empire (Ezra 7: 11–26). The same law book was subsequently read by Ezra and explained by Levites at a great open-air convocation in Jerusalem (Neh. 8–9). In later Jewish tradition, represented by 1 Esdras and the Talmud, Ezra came to be regarded as a figure of heroic proportions, a second Moses who restored the Pentateuch after it had been destroyed by the Babylonians. Historically, however, Ezra's law book cannot simply be equated with the Pentateuch, though it may have represented an important stage in the formation of Pentateuchal legislation.

In dealing with the related concepts of law and covenant the Chronicler is remarkable innovative. His historical narrative omits entirely the history of the period prior to the monarchy, and thus also the giving of the law at Sinai. It begins instead with the death of Saul and the accession of David. One consequence is that great prominence is given to the covenant with David (1 Chr. 17, based on 2 Sam. 7), the periodic renewal of which punctuates the history of the monarchy. Needless to say, the author does not eliminate or discount the Mosaic covenant but he follows the Priestly source in de-emphasizing it, probably with the idea that the Davidic covenant includes and subsumes the Mosaic. By the same token, David takes over the role of founding the temple cult and setting up its personnel. This shift of emphasis, which represents a surprising break with tradition, had the important effect of endowing royal decrees with divine authority. It could even serve to legitimate the measures taken by Ezra and Nehemiah, since both were emissaries of the Persian monarchy which considered itself juridically the successor to the Davidic dynasty.

A synoptic reading of the two versions of the Davidic covenant revealed by the prophet Nathan (2 Sam. 7 and 1 Chr. 17) will also show how the Chronicler, by introducing small changes into the text, has linked the covenant firmly with the building of the temple and the cult to be carried on in it. The shift is especially clear in the final word of promise:

Your house and your kingdom shall be made sure for ever before me.

(2 Sam. 7: 16)

I will confirm him in my house and in my kingdom for ever.

(1 Chr. 17: 14)

Here there is a very definite shift of emphasis from dynasty to temple; all the more remarkable, in that the earlier version stressed the divine promise of a house (meaning dynasty) over and against the human initiative of building a house (meaning temple). The Chronicler's point is demonstrated on a massive scale in his treatment of David's reign which occupies about one-fifth of the entire history (1 Chr. 11–29). The events emphasized are: the bringing of the ark of the covenant to Jerusalem where it was attended by Levites, the elaborate preparations made by David for the building of the temple, the establishment of the priests in their twenty-four courses (an arrangement unknown to the Pentateuch) and of the Levites, liturgical musicians, and others in their several divisions and guilds. For the Chronicler, therefore, David's chief claim to fame was not as warrior and founder of a dynasty but as the one who laid the foundations for temple worship. It is further implied that the dynastic promise was fulfilled primarily through the establishment of the cult which was the duty of his successors to maintain and, where necessary, restore to its original purity.

For the Chronicler the temple is the centre and focus of national life and the temple service the guarantee of order and well-being in the community. So important is it that he does not hesitate to amend the history to bring it into line with correct liturgical practice. Since, according to cultic law, only Levites could attend the ark, it had to be they who brought it up to Jerusalem during David's reign and ministered to it in its temporary resting place (1 Chr. 15–16). Since the king's sons could not be priests, as they are said to be at 2 Sam. 8: 18, they had to become chief officials instead (1 Chr. 18: 17). Levitical musicians had to play an important part in the dedication of Solomon's temple (2 Chr. 5: 11–13), though the class was not in existence at that time, and so on. In these and other respects the

Chronicler reads his own situation back into the time of the monarchy. A further example, noted earlier, is his account of Levites going from city to city during the reign of Jehoshaphat instructing the people in Torah with the help of a law book which they took with them (2 Chr. 17: 7–9).

Unlike the Priestly source, the Chronicler understood covenant to be a public act involving king and people which must be repeated at intervals, and especially after one of the rather frequent intervals of religious infidelity. The pattern was set during the reign of Asa, one of the early Judaean kings: a great assembly during which the people sacrificed, accepted the covenant with a binding oath, and carried out a purification of the cult and of religious life in general (2 Chr. 14: 3–5; 15: 9–15). The covenant and reform initiated by the priest Jehoiada on behalf of the young king Joash followed the same pattern. After the apostasy of Ahaz, an even more basic reform was carried out under Hezekiah whose renewal of the covenant was concluded with the celebration of Passover in Jerusalem (2 Chr. 29–31). During the reforms of Josiah yet another factor was introduced, i.e., the public reading of the law book recently discovered in the temple (2 Chr. 34). With this public reading the pattern of public assemblies in the Chronicler's own time was complete.

We have already noted the importance which the Chronicler attaches to the mission of Ezra as emissary of the Persian central government. Alarmed at the number of people in the Jerusalem community who had married foreign wives, Ezra convoked a plenary gathering to make a covenant sealed with an oath to remedy the matter once and for all. The narrative ends on a realistic note with the information that the meeting was rained off and the issue, so to speak, sent to committee (Ezra 10). Nehemiah 9–10 also records a plenary assembly at which the law was read, sins were confessed, and a written document drawn up and signed. By means of this solemn and official act the signatories bound themselves to observe the law, avoid 'mixed marriages', keep the law of sabbath and sabbatical year in all strictness, and contribute to the upkeep of temple worship. While the narrative implies that the entire Judaean community took part in this assembly, it seems more likely that this *written* covenant (9: 38) involved a more limited group which supported the reforms.

The impression given is almost of a sectarian setting, an anticipation of the solemn covenanting of the Qumran community.

For the Chronicler, at any rate, the decisive factor in the way the community understood itself and ordered its life was the existence of a *written* law. Assuming consistency in his reading of the history, this law book would be the one which was rediscovered during the reign of Josiah (2 Chr. 34). Since it was available and in use during the reign of Jehoshaphat more than two centuries earlier (2 Chr. 17: 7–9), he presumably wishes us to believe that it was forgotten or lost during the interval between Jehoshaphat and Josiah, perhaps during the dark days of Manasseh in the first half of the seventh century BCE. There can be no doubt that the author is referring to Deuteronomy, in whatever form it was known to him. In fact, on the only occasion when he cites 'the law, the book of Moses', the quotation is from the Deuteronomic law (2 Chr. 25: 4, cf. Deut. 24: 16). It was also, presumably, on the basis of the same law book that the diaspora community, newly returned from Babylon, restored religious life in the homeland (Ezra 3: 2; 6: 18). But there are indications too that he was also familiar with some at least of the cultic and ritual laws in Leviticus and Numbers. The feast of Tabernacles at the time of Ezra, for example, follows the calendric law in Leviticus rather than Deuteronomy (Neh. 8: 14–18). We observe here how the gradual development towards a comprehensive Torah, the Pentateuch as we have it, followed the evolving and expanding need for normative order in the post-exilic community.

It is also noteworthy that this law book is now the object of study and interpretation, the results of which are to be made available to the entire community. While the paradigm is Ezra, the priest and scribe, who 'had set his heart to study the law of Yahweh, and to do it, and to teach the statutes and ordinances in Israel' (Ezra 7: 10), the task of day-to-day instruction fell to the Levites. At the great assembly convened by Ezra, for the Chronicler an event of historic importance, the Levites not only helped Ezra read the law publicly but provided a running commentary:

The Levites helped the people to understand the law, while the people remained in their places. So they read from the book, from the law of God, with interpretation. They gave the sense, so that the people understood the reading. (Neh. 8: 7–8)

It is unfortunate that the meaning of the key words here translated as 'with interpretation' and 'gave the sense' is far from clear. Some have thought to find here the origin of the practice by which the Hebrew text was provided with a targum or paraphrase in the language of the people. This would assume that, by the time of Ezra's mission, or at least by the time of writing, the population in Jerusalem not only spoke Aramaic but no longer understood Hebrew. Since this is more than we know, it is safer to assume that what the Levites did was provide exposition of the law. This activity, known as *midrash halakah*, i.e., the discussion and exposition of the law with the purpose of establishing legal principles and handing down legal decisions, has remained one of the central characteristics of Jewish intellectual and religious life.

According to the perspective of this work, the law defines the community and determines who does or does not belong to it. What, then, is the community with which the author identifies? The genealogies in the first part of the work (1 Chr. 1–9) provide an initial clue with their progressive narrowing down from humanity as a whole to the descendants of Abraham, then to Judah and the line of David carried down to the time of writing. In retelling the history of the monarchy, the author omits almost all mention of the Northern Kingdom and represents the establishment of a separate cult at Bethel and Dan as a lapse into paganism, a worship of demons and satyrs who are 'no gods' (2 Chr. 13: 9), which historically was not the case at all. Thus the northern tribes and their descendants, the inhabitants of Samaria, are no longer part of the 'Israel of God'. The true Israel continued in Judah under Hezekiah, after the fall of the Northern Kingdom, constituting the 'remnant' that had escaped the Assyrian yoke and that came together in Jerusalem to celebrate a great Passover (2 Chr. 30). The parallelism with the other 'remnant' which returned from the Babylonian exile and celebrated Passover at the dedication of the temple is inescapable (Ezra 6: 19–22). It points to the author's conviction that it is through this group which went into exile, answered the call to return, rebuilt the temple, and re-established its worship unaided by the local population, that the legitimate line of descent is carried on. For the Chronicler, then, the true Israel is the community of those who returned from the Babylonian exile, the diaspora-group (Ezra 4: 1

etc.), the 'holy race' (Ezra 9: 2), which maintained and reinforced its distinctive character after the return, and especially after the reforms of Ezra and Nehemiah.

Historical objectivity requires us to add that this view of the Chronicler is polemical and one-sided. The many other Jews in the homeland and elsewhere who did not belong to this 'holy race' would no doubt have put it differently, but their opinions have not been allowed to survive. It has already been hinted that this kind of situation, with one group claiming to be the true Israel over against others, contains the seeds of sectarianism, even though sects are generally not thought to have emerged until much later in the Second Temple period.

We will, of course, bear in mind that the Chronicler's account of social and religious order based on temple worship and law represents only one of several perspectives in the emerging Judaism of the late Persian or early Hellenistic period. It is very much a clerical perspective, perhaps more specifically levitical, given the important role as teachers, preachers, and law experts assigned to Levites. The author, probably himself a Levite, has adopted some of the themes and literary procedures of the sages, but he follows the lead of Deuteronomy in a complete subordination of wisdom to law, intellectualism to morality. The tension between 'Greek wisdom' (secular learning) and Torah piety, submerged in the Chronicler's work, will become particularly acute during the subsequent two centuries.

Law and legal exposition in Jewish sectarianism

The Ezra–Nehemiah narrative records the existence of an élite group composed of those who had returned from the Babylonian diaspora, one which consciously set itself apart from other Jews in the province of Judah. By means of a special covenant and oath this group dedicated itself to a strict interpretation of the law as they understood it, with special reference to intermarriage, sabbath, and the upkeep of the temple (Neh. 9: 38—10: 39). The making of covenants of this kind, with the precise stipulations and even the names of the signatories in writing, marks a stage in the development which would lead to sectarianism, precisely by emphasizing the nonascriptive and contractual basis for membership in a particular group. The groundwork for the development of sects was laid with the breakup of the state and the emergence of different centres in the homeland and diaspora claiming continuity with the past. With the development of an in-group mentality in any such centre, allied with the conviction that it alone embodies the 'true Israel', we can begin to speak of sects. This explains why such groups, when they achieve distinct social visibility, refer to themselves by such designations as the 'holy covenant', 'the sons of the covenant', and the like.

We noted a moment ago how the Chronicler attests to the growing importance of legal exposition. Once we pass to a written law as the decisive instrument of public order, those professionally responsible for its interpretation are bound to exercise increasing influence. The Chronicler restricts this task largely if not exclusively to Levites. Eventually, it would be shared by laymen, due in part to the loss of prestige of the temple clergy, and in part to Pharisee influence. (We recall the frequent allusion in the gospels to 'scribes and Pharisees'.) Writing in the early second century BCE, Ben Sira attests that the scribe was first and foremost a legal scholar with the responsibility of teaching others:

> How different is the one who devotes himself
> to the study of the law of the Most High!
> He seeks out the wisdom of all the ancients;
> and is concerned with prophecies . . .
> He will show the wisdom of what he has learned,
> and will glory in the law of Yahweh's covenant.
> (Ecclus. 39: 1, 8)

By Ben Sira's day the synagogue provided a centre for both prayer and study in addition to private academies such as the one for which the author does a little advertising at the end of his book:

> Draw near to me, you who are uneducated,
> and lodge in my school. (51: 23)

In spite of the great gaps in our knowledge of Jewish life in the fourth and third centuries BCE, it is reasonable to suppose that some of the legal learning and exposition of that time has survived in the corpus of legal material codified in the Mishnah almost four centuries later. In the one tractate with attributions, *m.Aboth*, several of the sages mentioned lived no more than a generation or so after the time of Ben Sira.

Ben Sira represents a fairly mainline position, but legal exposition was also going on in dissident groups. The little we know about them indicates a remarkable variety with respect both to the claims underlying their particular brand of interpretation and the positions adopted on different subjects. It is important to emphasize this variety, since in Judaism, as also in Christianity, the uniformity achieved or imposed by religious orthodoxy has tended to dominate our understanding of the past.

The standard view according to which Jewish sectarianism first emerged in the second century BCE, with the well-known triad of Pharisees, Sadducees, and Essenes of Josephus, is in need of revision. Much, of course, depends on how one defines the term 'sect', but we have texts from the early Persian period which certainly sound sectarian in character. Take, for example, an apostrophe from the last section of Isaiah, generally dated to that time:

> Hear the word of Yahweh,
>   you who tremble at his word:
> Your own people who hate you
>   and reject you for my name's sake
> have said, 'let Yahweh be glorified,
>   so that we may see your joy';
> but it is they who shall be put to shame.   (Isa. 66: 5)

This word of comfort comes from an anonymous seer and is addressed to a despised minority within the Jewish polity which has been 'excommunicated' on account of their association with the seer, whose eschatological expectations are rejected by the majority, and who see themselves, and themselves alone, as 'the saved'. In the account of Ezra's campaign against 'mixed marriages' (Ezra 9–10) he was supported by 'those who tremble at the commandment of our God' (Ezra 10: 3, cf. 9: 4), in other words, by pietists closely related to, if not identical with, the 'quakers' of Isa. 66: 5. We would therefore have evidence for a prophetic–eschatological group in the mid-fifth century which also hewed to a strict interpretation of the law—too strict, in fact, since we know of no law, Israelite or Persian, mandating divorce in any circumstances.

The conquests of Alexander placed Palestinian Jews under the rule of kings and courts which were Greek in language and culture: first, the Ptolemies in the third century who ruled from Alexandria in Egypt; then the Seleucids in Antioch in Syria who followed them. After more than half a century of rule, the latter were obliged to grant a measure of independence to Judaea in 142 BC. The dominance of the Greek way of life, with its strong drive to cultural homogeneity, resulted inevitably in the erosion of religious traditions and local cults all over the vast empire created by Alexander. Since Greek religion was intimately part of civic life, with sacrifices accompanying every kind of public act, it was practically impossible for those Jews living in cities to aspire to the professions or to public office without in some way compromising their faith.

In the course of time such typically Greek institutions as the theatre, ephebion (youth centre), and gymnasium were established in Jerusalem itself. Schools embodying the humanistic ideals of Greek education (*paideia*) inevitably exerted a considerable attraction. One has only to read Qoheleth who, as we saw earlier, is conversant with philosophical currents of the Ptolemaic age and never mentions Torah. The situation was, in some respects, similar to that in which European Jews were to find themselves during the European Enlightenment. The available options can easily be detailed. One could embrace the new world-view and bring laws into conformity with it; one could reject that world-view out of hand, insisting on a more rigorous interpretation of the laws; or, the course no doubt taken by most, one could make whatever pragmatic accommodations seemed to be called for without feeling obliged to take a clear stand.

This last option became more difficult to maintain after the accession of the Seleucid king Antiochus IV Epiphanes in 175 BCE. At first favourable to the large Jewish population in his kingdom, Antiochus was soon driven by desperate financial need to impose heavy taxation and even plunder the temple treasury. By 167 BCE matters came to a head with a royal decree of unification which, in effect, proscribed the Jewish religion. This was followed by the establishment of the cult of Zeus, patron deity of the dynasty, in the Jerusalem temple. This first 'final solution of the Jewish problem' provoked its reaction in armed rebellion and guerrilla warfare which, under the leadership of the Maccabee family, led to the reoccupation of Jerusalem (with the exception of the citadel), the cleansing of the temple and, eventually, a considerable measure of independence.

While this persecution was only too real, it is important to note that the chain of events leading to it began with a crisis internal to the Jewish community. We get hints of it in Ben Sira, writing a few years before the accession of Antiochus, where he condemns hypocrites who 'stumble over the law' (Ecclus. 32: 15) and an ungodly people who have forsaken it (41: 8). In context, this would refer to those who were accommodating the law to contemporary culture inspired by Greek ideals. Our principal source for the Antiochean crisis, 1 Maccabees written about 100 BCE, is quite explicit on this point:

In those days [i.e. after the accession of Antiochus] certain renegades came out from Israel and misled many, saying, 'Let us go and make a covenant with the Gentiles around us, for since we separated from them many disasters have come upon us.' This proposal pleased them, and some of the people eagerly went to the king, who authorized them to observe the ordinances of the Gentiles. So they built a gymnasium in Jerusalem, according to Gentile custom, and removed the marks of circumcision, and abandoned the holy covenant. They joined with the Gentiles and sold themselves to do evil. (1 Macc. 1: 11–15)

It is natural that the author, writing as an apologist for the Maccabees and the Hasmonaean principate which they founded, should represent these opponents as simply abandoning Judaism for a Gentile lifestyle. More probably, however, these 'Hellenizers', led by priestly families including that of the high priest himself, had evolved their own understanding of the law so as to allow for a large area of accommodation to contemporary Greek culture. Some may have gone so far as to deny the divine origin of the Mosaic law, putting it on the same footing as other codes, those of Lycurgus and Solon, for example. Others would have been content to argue that certain more specifically Jewish features of the law, such as circumcision, sabbath rest, food taboos, were later accretions which should be abandoned as mere superstition. They could even have found arguments for accepting or at least tolerating the worship of Zeus since, from the earliest days of the settlement in the land, Yahweh had been seen by some to be an alternative embodiment of one of the gods of Canaan. After all, had not Abraham sworn to Melchizedek by Yahweh-El Elyon (Gen. 14: 22)?

Our principal source describes the conservative reaction to these measures and the persecution to which they led:

Many in Israel stood firm and were resolved in their hearts not to eat unclean food. They chose to die rather than to be defiled by food or to profane the holy covenant; and they did die. And very great wrath came upon Israel. (1 Macc. 1: 62–3)

It could be argued that there were more important things in Torah than the food laws but these, together with circumcision and sabbath, had been elevated to confessional status. 2 Maccabees, based on a five-volume history by Jason of Cyrene written in the first century BCE, gives a more detailed account of these first Jewish martyrdoms: women hurled from the city walls for circumcising their children, others burnt alive for secretly observing sabbath, an aged scribe tortured to death for refusing to eat pork (6: 7–31). For the author of 1 Maccabees, the first organized resistance came from the country priest Matthias and his sons (2: 1–28) who are described as fighting for the sanctuary and the law (14: 29). But he also speaks of 'many who were seeking righteousness and justice' who retired with their families into the Judaean wilderness and who, when confronted by the Seleucid forces on the sabbath, refused to fight and were promptly slaughtered (2: 29–38). Their sacrifice, which was prompted by fidelity to the law and not by pacifism, led to an important modification of the sabbath law permitting those attacked on the sabbath to resist (2: 39–41).

The same author goes on to mention another group called Asidaeans (corresponding to the Hebrew *ḥasidim*, meaning devout or faithful) who joined forces with Mattathias and his sons. They are described as a 'company' (literally 'synagogue'), warriors who offered themselves for the law, opponents of the renegades or Hellenizers whom they attacked without mercy (2: 42–4). They may be the same as the 'assembly of the faithful' who fought alongside Judas Maccabee at the battle of Beth-horon (3: 13). We meet them again a little later, together with a company of scribes negotiating terms of peace with the Seleucid general Bacchides and the newly appointed high priest Alcimus (Yakim), an incident which ended with the latter treacherously slaughtering sixty of their number (7: 12–18).

From these allusions we may deduce that the Asidaeans formed an identifiable group or association committed to the strict observance of the law and counting among their number those whose task it was to interpret it. Since they were prepared to seek terms once the anti-Jewish edict had been repealed (6: 58–9), their stake in the struggle was clearly quite different from that of the Maccabees. They must also have attached great importance to the legitimacy of the high priestly office since they were led to negotiate by the appointment of one who, though no better than his predecessors, was at least of genuine Aaronite descent (7: 14).

The last point is important for understanding the sequence of events which led to the emergence of the named sects in the last two and a half centuries of the Second Temple. After the accession of Antiochus IV, the high priest Onias III was deposed and his place taken by Jason (Jesus) his brother who paid the new king handsomely for the favour. Not long afterwards, however, Jason was outbid by a certain Menelaus (Menahem), an even more enthusiastic devotee of the Greek way of life. More ominously, he was not even of legitimate Aaronite–Zadokite stock as required by the law. Alcimus, his successor, was at least an Aaronite and thus could command some measure of tolerance. By that time, however, a fatal precedent had been set whereby the Gentile ruler filled the high priesthood with the highest bidder. The way was therefore prepared for Jonathan, brother and successor of Judas, to accept the offer from Alexander Balas, usurper of the Seleucid throne, and for his successor Simon to be confirmed in the office:

The Jews and their priests decided that Simon should be their leader and high priest for ever, until a trustworthy prophet should arise.

(1 Macc. 14: 41)

From what we have learned of the Asidaeans (Hasidim), we must conclude that they would have rejected this move out of hand. This, if anything, was the decisive issue leading to the schism and the formation of sects in the strict sense of the term.

Several scholars have identified either Jonathan or Simon with the

Wicked Priest of the Qumran scrolls who opposed the Teacher of Righteousness, founder and leader of the sect. It was, at any rate, on this crucial point of the legitimacy of the high priesthood that the Qumran sect, and possibly others, distanced themselves from the temple personnel and its services.

Internal evidence suggests that, in its final form, Daniel was written after the setting up of the altar to Olympian Zeus in the temple in December 167 BCE (it is referred to as 'the abomination that makes desolate' in the book, 11: 31 and 12: 11) and before the rededication of the temple exactly three years later. The court tales in the first part of the book (to be discussed in greater detail in Ch. 6) probably circulated earlier than the visions, though they are quite closely linked with them. It is not difficult to see how they could have served to strengthen the faith of those who were suffering persecution. Daniel and his companions observed the food laws (1: 8–16), prayed three times a day (6: 10), and rejected idolatry even at the risk of their lives (chs. 3 and 6). Like the visions that follow, the tales move in an atmosphere of divine mysteries, esoteric lore, dream interpretation, communion with angels, and intense piety. The communications which the seer receives in visions promise an end to present tribulations. In the coded language of apocalyptic, they trace the course of events up to and beyond the time of writing, concluding with precise calculations of the imminent end of history and the coming of God's kingdom.

The author of Daniel clearly identified himself with those who were suffering persecution (11: 33–4) and dissociated himself from 'the men of violence among your own people' (11: 14), presumably the Hellenizers who supported Antiochus. The faithful addressed by him are 'the saints of the Most High' (7: 18, 21–2, 25) and 'the wise' (11: 33, 35; 12: 3, 10), though it is possible that the latter refers more specifically to the leaders of the group. That the apocalyptic seer's audience is the Asidaean assembly of 1 Maccabees is widely accepted and entirely plausible. The 'little help' which the persecuted are said to receive, and the adhesion to their cause of dubious allies (11: 34), would then refer to the Maccabees and their associates who joined the struggle *after* the persecution was under way. Since the statement that the tyrant will be broken by no human hand (8: 25) does not necessarily imply a pacifist or quietist posture, there is no incompatibility with the warlike character of the Asidaeans who, in any case, fought only by necessity and for much more limited objectives than the Maccabees.

Daniel, then, was written in and for an apocalyptic sect dedicated to upholding the holy covenant and the laws, practising its own kind of biblical interpretation (e.g. the author's reinterpretation of the seventy years of Jeremiah, Dan. 9: 1–2), and following its own sectarian *halakah* (legal interpretation). As such, it stands somewhere between the diaspora-group which supported the reforms of Ezra and the Qumran community established around the middle of the second century BCE.

On the origins of the sects mentioned by Josephus (Essenes, Pharisees, Sadducees) there is much uncertainty. While the precise sequence of events is unknown, the Essenes probably originated as a branch of Asidaeans who broke with the Maccabee leadership after Jonathan assumed the high priestly office around the middle of the second century BCE. As described by the Jewish authors Josephus and Philo and the Roman naturalist Pliny the Elder, they formed communities of ascetics both in the cities and in the Judaean wilderness by the Dead Sea. Their lives were governed by a strict interpretation of the laws, especially the laws of purity, in addition to which they cherished their own esoteric teachings which they were bound by the most solemn oaths not to disclose. Most scholars identify the community of the Qumran scrolls as a branch of the Essenes, though several other candidates (including Jewish-Christians) have been proposed. The writings recovered from the caves since 1947, especially the community rules, confirm that the principal activity of the group was the study of Torah, which served as a substitute for participation in temple worship. Their founder, the Teacher of Righteousness (or the Legitimate Teacher) was above all a faithful interpreter of the law, and the task of authoritative legal exposition was continued by the Zadokite priests who formed the leadership. As in the days of Ezra and Nehemiah, the members entered into a covenant confirmed by oath:

Whoever approaches the Council of the Community shall enter the Covenant of God in the presence of all who have freely pledged themselves. He shall undertake by a binding oath to return with all his heart and soul to every commandment of the Law of Moses in accordance with all that has been revealed of it to the sons of Zadok, the Keepers of the Covenant and Seeker of His will, and to the multitude of the men of their Covenant who together have freely pledged themselves to His truth and to walking in the way of His delight. And he shall undertake by the Covenant to separate from all the men of falsehood who walk in the way of wickedness. (Community Rule 5: 7–11)

It is important to note that the members committed themselves not just to Torah in general but to a particular interpretation of the laws. Something of this sectarian *halakah* can be found in the community rules, especially the Damascus Document, so called on account of the allusion in it to a new covenant made in the land of Damascus, possibly a symbolic name for Qumran. The sect's interpretation is, in general, stricter than that of the Pharisees, especially with regard to sabbath and ritual cleanliness. While, for example, the Pharisees would allow an animal to be pulled out of a pit on the sabbath (see Matt. 12: 11), the Damascus Rule forbade it (11: 13–14). The most recently published and the longest of the Qumran texts, the Temple Scroll containing sixty-seven columns, goes to extreme lengths to preserve not only the temple precincts but also the entire city from any taint of ritual impurity. To cite only one example: a man who has had sexual relations with his wife must wait three days to enter the holy city (col. 45: 11–12). It is clear that, for the sectarians, these stipulations were on the same level as Pentateuchal law. One of the most surprising aspects of the Temple Scroll is that it contains, in effect, an *emended* version of parts of the Deuteronomic law attributed not, as in Deuteronomy, to Moses but directly to God himself.

The Temple Scroll provides one example among many of the remarkable variety of interpretative positions with respect to the law in the late Second Temple period. We find a quite different perspective among the Pharisees whose early history is, unfortunately, not well known. As far as we can tell, they constituted a predominantly lay movement which emerged from the matrix of Hasidism during the early Hasmonaean period, though probably later than the Essenes. Reacting to the widespread secularization of the priesthood, the Pharisees (the word probably means 'separatists') sought to apply the purity laws encumbent on the priesthood to the entire people, and thus to realize the ideal of a 'kingdom of priests, a holy nation' (Exod. 19: 6). They were organized in associations based on table fellowship—the table standing for the altar—and were committed to laws governing diet, tithing, purity, and conduct in general. The Pharisees were not on principle opposed to the priesthood —indeed, several priests joined their ranks—but the movement marked a decisive shift towards a lay religion which has characterized Judaism, and differentiated it from Christianity, ever since.

In pursuit of their ideals, the Pharisees engaged in a campaign of religious education, recruiting disciples and teaching in the synagogues around the land. Some important aspects of the way in which they understood themselves and their mission are captured in the opening sentence of the Mishnaic treatise 'The Sayings of the Fathers' (*m.Aboth*):

Moses received Torah from Sinai and delivered it to Joshua; then Joshua to the elders, the elders to the prophets, and the prophets delivered it to the men of the Great Assembly. They said three things: be deliberate in judgement, raise up many disciples, and make a hedge for the Torah.

These three injunctions correspond to important functions of the scribe in the last days of the Second Temple: counsel in the administration of justice, teaching, and legal exposition. The 'hedge' is the complex of legal exegesis which safeguards the integrity of the biblical laws and, at the same time, applies them realistically to the actual situations of everyday life.

We should not be misled by the anti-Pharisaic polemic in the gospels into misrepresenting the intent and the effect of this teaching. As is now generally recognized, much of this polemic reflects the growing alienation between the Christian movement and the Jewish leadership which led to the Jewish–Christian schism in the decades following the great war with Rome. As against the Sadducees, who insisted on the letter of the law supplemented by their own decrees, the Pharisees developed a wide-ranging and complex *halakah* the purpose of which was to apply the laws humanely to concrete situations. The goal, we might say, was to make the law really work, and thus to bring the whole of life into conformity with the will of God. The measure of success achieved by this programme will be appreciated when we recall that it survived the disastrous wars with Rome to give shape and character to Jewish life in the reconstruction which followed.

6

Theological Wisdom

The confluence of wisdom and law

At the end of the first chapter the reader was invited to think of wisdom and law as two great rivers which eventually flow together and find their outlet in rabbinic writings and early Christian theology. At different points in their development also, the sapiential and legal traditions mingle together or follow parallel courses. We saw, for example, some interesting formal similarities between case law and proverbial sayings, and between apodictic sentences of law and the instruction. These led to the suggestion that, in its earliest stages, Israelite law could be seen as a specialization of clan wisdom. We also noted that all the different compilations of laws contain more than just legal enactments. Our brief study of these collections, all the way from the Covenant Code to the Damascus Rule and Temple Scroll from Qumran, has shown that they cannot be described purely and simply as law codes. In their care to provide appropriate motivation for observing the laws and to promote a reflective approach to the moral life in general, they come close in several respects to the teaching of the sages.

The same observation holds for the tendency to generalize, to state the essence of the laws in a few basic principles or norms, a tendency which we have noted throughout our study. When the great Hillel reduced the 613 laws of the Pentateuch to the Golden Rule, or when Jesus, in answer to a lawyer's question, expressed the essence of the law in the command to love God and the neighbour (Matt. 22: 34–40), they were simply following a precedent set by the prophets and the sages. This would suggest that the teaching of the sages entered the mainstream of Israelite religion at the point where it came together with the legal tradition.

We saw, too, that the publication of Deuteronomy marked an important point in the process which brought these two traditions together to form a kind of intellectual tradition unique in the ancient world. Since many influences and many interests converged in Deuteronomy, it cannot simply be described as a product of scribalism; but scribes or 'handlers of the law' must have had a hand in it, and its emphasis on teaching and instruction brings to mind the practice of the sages. When Israel observes the laws it is recognized as a wise nation (Deut. 4: 6–7) and when it neglects them it is guilty of folly (32: 28–9). With regard to the understanding of wisdom, the book also contains a hint of later developments where it describes the law as revealed and accessible:

Surely, this commandment that I am commanding you today is not too hard for you, nor is it too far away. It is not in heaven, that you should say, 'Who will go up to heaven for us, and get it for us, so that we may hear it and observe it?' Neither is it beyond the sea, that you should say, 'Who will cross to the other side of the sea for us, and get it for us, so that we may hear it and observe it?' No, the word is very near to you; it is in your mouth and in your heart for you to observe

(Deut. 30: 11–14)

So there is a hidden wisdom, an esoteric knowledge, which God has not chosen to reveal, and which should not be sought in heaven (i.e. in esoteric speculation) or overseas (i.e. in the wisdom of other lands), a wisdom over against the knowledge of the law which he *has* revealed and which is all the wisdom Israel needs. The distinction is explicit at a different point in Moses' final address:

The secret things belong to Yahweh our God, but the revealed things belong to us and to our children forever, to observe all the words of this law. (29: 29)

Deuteronomy is at the beginning of a certain distancing from secular learning, what will later be called 'Greek wisdom', a withdrawal into an intellectualism which has as its goal the perfecting of the moral life. There is also contained here, by implication, a perception of the nature of wisdom which would generate new insights and problems. The true wisdom is a divine prerogative which is available to humankind only as God chooses to reveal it. As the author sees it, that part of divine wisdom which he has chosen to reveal is contained in the law. The law is therefore *the* expression of divine wisdom made available to Israel and, as such, can compete on more than equal terms with the vaunted wisdom of the nations. Nothing is said about the 'secret things' or, in other words, that part of wisdom which remains hidden with God, to which the writers of apocalyptic tracts will claim to be privy. Nor is anything said about any disposition made by God for the guidance of those outside Israel. We must now go on to see how these issues were developed by scribes and sages of the Second Temple period. Since an exhaustive analysis is clearly impossible, we shall concentrate on a few texts which reflect more directly on the nature of wisdom and attempt to follow up whatever leads they may offer us.

Job 28: inaccessible wisdom

In the context of the debate as it now stands, the poem on wisdom in Job 28 is part of a discourse assigned to Job himself (27: 1). But the passage immediately preceding the poem (27: 13–23) contains a vivid description of how the evildoer gets his comeuppance, which could hardly have been spoken by Job, who has expended a great deal of his energy in denying precisely that this is what happens. More probably, then, it belongs to the third contribution of Zophar which, as we saw earlier, has been somewhat scrambled in transmission. Several commentators have also argued, or simply stated, that the poem in chapter 28 was originally an independent composition, and that it has been provided with a conclusion more consonant with orthodox piety (28: 28). For that conclusion, which equates wisdom with the fear of Yahweh or, in other words, religious observance, seems inappropriate coming from Job at that point in the book, and does not make an easy fit with the rest of the poem either.

Using the powerful metaphor of mining, the poet begins by describing the labour involved in obtaining silver, gold, iron, copper, and precious ore of all kinds: working long hours underground, far from the haunts of everyday life, in constant danger and, above all, in isolation:

That path no bird of prey knows,
  and the falcon's eye has not seen it.
The proud wild animals have not trodden it;
  the lion has not passed over it.   (28: 7–8)

The genesis of the image may, perhaps, be found in those proverbs
and instructions which compare wisdom with precious metals:

Happy are those who find wisdom,
  and those who get understanding,
for her income is better than silver,
  and her revenue better than gold.
She is more precious than jewels,
  and nothing you desire can compare with her.
                                    (Prov. 3: 13–15)

The point is that if such a price must be paid to obtain precious metals from the earth, how much more difficult must it be to acquire
wisdom? There is no comforting answer to the question which is
then posed as a refrain in the poem:

Where shall wisdom be found?
  and where is the place of understanding?   (Job 28: 12, 20)

It is not in the land of the living, nor in the heights and depths of
the cosmos, nor in the dark waters with which the Hebrew imagination surrounded the inhabited world. There exists no currency
with which it may be purchased or against which it may even be
appraised. Even Death, who presides over all, has heard but a
rumour of it (v. 22).

The conclusion of the poem is that only God knows and possesses
wisdom since only he was present at the Creation when he saw,
appraised, and approved it (vv. 23–7). This image of wisdom present
with God in the act of creation is consonant with the mythological
scenario described in God's answer to Job out of the whirlwind (Job
38: 4–7). We saw earlier how the cosmos can be imagined as a great
temple and its construction, at Creation, can be rounded off with a
ceremony of dedication at which the 'sons of God', members of the
divine retinue, engage with joyful song in the liturgy. The earthly
counterpart is, of course, the dedication of Solomon's temple (1 Kgs.
8) and of the rebuilt temple after the return from exile (Ezra 3:

10–13). There is therefore in the poem at least a hint of wisdom personified participating in some way in the work of creation, a hint which will be more fully developed in another composition to be considered shortly (Prov. 8: 22–31).

After this strong statement about the unsuccessful search for wisdom in the world, the finale may sound rather anticlimactic and even incongruous:

> And he said to humankind,
> 'Truly, the fear of Yahweh, that is wisdom;
>   and to depart from evil is understanding.'   (v. 28)

Most commentators conclude that these lines have been added as a sort of nervous corrective to the negative verdict on the human quest for wisdom in the body of the poem. After all, it was axiomatic with the sages that the search for wisdom would not go unrewarded:

> If you seek it like silver
>   and search for it as for hidden treasures;
> then you will understand the fear of Yahweh,
>   and find the knowledge of God.   (Prov. 2: 4)

It is also worth noting that the same language of fearing Yahweh and turning from evil occurs in the narrative prologue where Yahweh turns to the Satan and says:

Have you considered my servant Job? There is no one like him on the earth, a blameless and upright man, *who fears God and turns away from evil.* (1: 8, emphasis added)

This might suggest that the same author who provided the dialogue with its narrative framework also felt it necessary to end the poem in a way consonant with the final form of the book. That this was the conventional solution may be seen in an admonition in Proverbs which might have been written expressly for Job (italics mine):

> Trust in Yahweh with all your heart,
>   and do not rely on your own insight.
> In all your ways acknowledge him,
>   and he will make straight your paths.
> Do not be wise in your own eyes;
>   *fear Yahweh and turn away from evil.*

> It will be a healing for your flesh
> > and a refreshment for your body.   (3: 5–8)

This answer of conventional piety which, faithful to the perspectives of Deuteronomy, equates wisdom with doing good and avoiding evil, and therefore, in effect, with observing law, makes a point which is by no means trivial. Given the problematic nature of experience it is not, however, a completely adequate answer. That, as we have seen, is the whole point of the dialogue in Job. If, then, we turn to consider the poem in its original form, without the 'orthodox' ending, we can see how it could have functioned as a criticism of Job who, misled by the rationalist creed of the sages to whose ranks he belonged, assumed that the problems posed by experience should always yield to intellectual enquiry. If, however, the author of Job meant to attribute the poem to Zophar, it would have served as an indictment of Job's refusal to accept the mysterious ways of God. It would be a reminder both to him and to his colleagues that the kind of wisdom necessary for solving the problem posed by his experience, for reducing it to some semblance of rationality, was simply not available.

If this interpretation is correct, it is really not very important to decide whether the poem was interpolated or not. Much of the imagery is, in any case, found elsewhere in the book, and Job's partners in dialogue refer more than once to divine wisdom manifested in creation (e.g. 26: 5–14; 36: 24–33; 37: 1–24). Zophar himself had already made the same point, with the same implications, in a somewhat different way:

> Oh, that God would speak,
> > and open his lips to you,
> and that he would tell you the secrets of wisdom!
> > for wisdom is many-sided . . .
> Can you find out the deep things of God?
> > Can you find out the limits of the Almighty?
> It is higher than heaven—what can you do?
> > Deeper than Sheol—what can you know?   (11: 5–8)

Zophar's prayer was answered and God did speak; but he said nothing which had not been said already in the book (38: 1—40: 2). If Job was satisfied, it was not because of what was said, but because of who said it:

I had heard of you by the hearing of the ear,
but now my eye sees you . . . (42: 5)

The world-wide search for wisdom of which the poem speaks is consonant with the practice, common to the sages, of interrogating nature for clues to rational order and analogies to the moral life. It is now becoming clear to many, however, including the author of the poem, that this whole procedure has become quite problematic. Nature does not so easily render up its secrets to human reason confident of its own powers. On the contrary, it itself poses questions which call for a deeper level of reflection.

Proverbs 8: 22–31: Wisdom, first-born of creation

Proverbs 1–9, discussed briefly in an earlier chapter, is often taken to be the work of whoever put together the several components of the book. It is, in any case, one of the most recent of these components. It was placed at the beginning as a kind of theological preface to the book as a whole, to which the acrostic poem on the 'valiant woman' at the end corresponds. The intent was to bind together and consolidate the scattershot aphoristic wisdom in the book into an intellectually coherent whole by subsuming it under a theoretical concept encapsulated in a female personification. It will be interesting to see how this was done.

Proverbs 1–9 consists of a series of instructions given by the 'father' (i.e. the sage), most of which are introduced by an appeal to 'the son' (i.e. the student) to listen and take the teaching to heart. Depending on how one identifies the individual units, there are some sixteen to eighteen including instructions, admonitions, colourful descriptions of evildoers involved in murder and mayhem, lurid descriptions of the seductive woman—the usual stock-in-trade of moral didacticism. Where wisdom, i.e. the teaching of the master, is described, there is an understandable tendency to use the language of personification, and since the Hebrew word for 'wisdom' (*hokmah*) is feminine, wisdom has the attributes of a good and desirable woman. As such, she is more precious than pearls or jewels (3: 15; 8: 11), she can be grasped in a loving embrace (3: 18; 4: 8), and, to top it all, she has her own house (9: 1–6), is well-off, and promises prosperity (3: 14; 8: 18).

The tendency to endow abstract qualities with personal attributes is quite natural and well-attested, for example, in ancient Greece (e.g. *nemesis*, retribution; *tyke*, fortune, fate). Female personifications were familiar in Israel as, for example, virgin Israel, daughter of Zion, and helped to introduce a broad range of affectivity into the language, dealing with such themes as erotic desire and affection between spouses. Some scholars have argued that the Woman called Wisdom in Proverbs 1–9 is modelled on a Canaanite female wisdom deity. We shall see that this can be a productive line of enquiry, even though evidence for the existence of such a deity is lacking. But first we must look at the two passages in Proverbs 1–9 in which Wisdom herself speaks (1: 20–33; 8: 1–36).

In the first of these she addresses the uninstructed in the market place or the city gate, or anywhere where people tend to forgather. Since she speaks in her own person, and yet speaks for Yahweh, it is clear that her discourse is modelled on prophetic speech and that she herself is a prophet. We can compare her language of calling out to an unresponsive audience with examples taken from late prophecy:

> Because I have called and you refused,
>   have stretched out my hand and no one heeded,
> and because you have ignored all my counsel
>   and would have none of my reproof,
> I also will laugh at your calamity . . .
>
> Then they will call upon me, but I will not answer;
>   they will seek me diligently but they will not find me . . .
>   (Prov. 1: 24–6, 28)
>
> Then you shall call, and Yahweh will answer;
>   you shall cry for help, and he will say, Here I am.
>
> I was ready to be sought out by those who did not ask,
>   to be found by those who did not seek me.
> I said, 'Here I am, here I am,'
>   to a nation that did not call on my name.
>   (Isa. 58: 9; 65: 1)

The same kind of speech is continued in Proverbs 8: 1–21 which, however, deals largely with the workings of wisdom in the social and political sphere. The mixture of the sapiential and prophetic in these passages is another pointer to the take-over of the prophetic role by the sages as a way of enhancing the authority of their teaching. A similar claim is heard occasionally in the Job debate (e.g. Job 4: 12–21) and Ben Sira, somewhat implausibly, compares his teaching to prophecy (Ecclus. 24: 33). Later still, the rabbis will claim that prophecy has been taken from the prophets and given to the sages (e.g. in b.Baba Bathra 12*a*).

While the Woman called Wisdom does not seem to be presented in the guise of a goddess, it is perfectly possible that she was conceived as a counter to the baleful influence of the Foreign or, more precisely, Outsider Woman, who would therefore be the primary symbolic figure in these chapters (2: 16–19; 5: 3–23; 6: 24–35; 7: 5–27; 9: 13–18). This need not surprise, since the Woman called Wisdom embodies the sage's teaching and, as such, functions precisely to counter deviant and transgressive religious and moral conduct. The Outsider Woman's seductive arts are described graphically, not to say luridly, and in some detail. There is even the motif, common to ancient and modern fiction, of the husband absent on business (7: 19–20). We would therefore be led to think of this portrait as serving the purpose of moral admonition, and, indeed, the point about marital infidelity is made explicitly and in moralizing terms (5: 15–20; 6: 25–35). If, however, we recall the frequent association in the Hebrew Bible between sexual immorality and idolatry (e.g. 1 Kgs. 11: 1–9 and Hos. 1–3), we shall see that this portrait of the *femme fatale* also stands for the allure of foreign cults and therefore warns against *religious* infidelity. One has only to think of the foreign wives of Esau or Solomon or the measures taken by Ezra against marriages with women outside the civic–religious community.

A comparison of the two figures will show that the character, attributes, and activities of the Woman called Wisdom form a reverse image of those of the Outsider Woman. Both offer love, but of a very different kind, both can be addressed as lover or bride (e.g. 7: 4), both can be grasped and embraced (3: 1, 8; 4: 8; 5: 20), but while contact with the one is life-enhancing, the other is death-dealing, literally a *femme fatale*. Each has her house, to which she invites the youth, but for quite different purposes. Wisdom (*hokmah*) is presented with all the positive aspects of femininity. Like the good woman described at the end of the book, she is 'more precious than pearls' (31: 10, cf. 3: 15; 8: 11; Job 28: 18), a phrase which seems to have been proverbial in Israel for a good wife.

The second discourse of Wisdom takes a quite different and unexpected direction (8: 22–31); so much so, that several commentators have felt obliged to conclude that it embodies a more mature and advanced way of thinking and therefore must have been interpolated. Wisdom declares that she came into existence at the beginning of Creation and that she was present with God during the work of creation. There is a certain studied ambiguity in speaking of *how* Wisdom came into existence, owing to the fact that the poet is taking over and adapting a theogony, a type of myth which speaks of the genealogy and birth of gods and goddesses. It is also less than clear what role, if any, Wisdom played in the work of creation. The Greek translator, followed by RSV, interprets the end of the passage in the sense that Wisdom acted as God's agent and artificer:

> then I was beside him, like a master worker;
> and I was daily his delight,
>   rejoicing before him always,
> rejoicing in his inhabited world
>   and delighting in the human race.   (8: 30–1)

In other words, she was commissioned to do the work in much the same way that Moses commissioned Bezalel, an artificer full of the Spirit and of wisdom (Exod. 35: 31), to make the wilderness sanctuary and its furniture. But this line of interpretation seems to ignore the context which conveys rather the image of a favourite child who delights her father and takes pleasure in what he has made. Here, too, the obscurity may be due to the inappropriate representation of Yahweh as a god who begets offspring, which would have seemed quite inappropriate.

The literary form, according to which something or someone is created *before* a series of other things (8: 22–6), is a first clue to the mythic character of this representation. It can be verified, for example, in the opening of the canonical Babylonian Creation myth (called *enuma elish* from its opening words) and is reflected in the introduction to the Eden myth in Genesis—when there were no plants, no grass, no rain, no farmer to till the soil, *then* God cre-

ated . . . (2: 4–5). Since Wisdom is a person begotten at the beginning of time, the specific form of the myth is a theogony, amply
attested in ancient Mesopotamia, Egypt, and Greece. The closest
parallel known to us from cultures familiar to Israel and early
Judaism is the Egyptian myth of the birth of the goddess Maat from
the sun god Re. His favourite child, she came down to humankind
at the beginning of time as the embodiment of cosmic order and the
preserver of law and justice. During the Hellenistic period Maat was
identified with the great Egyptian goddess Isis whose cult was
extremely popular throughout the Mediterranean world, nowhere
more so than in the Ptolemaic empire to which Judah belonged during the third century BCE. Since this provides a quite plausible date
for the poem, there seems no good reason to deny the possibility of
such a borrowing.

What we find, then, in Proverbs 8: 22–31 is a reflective use of
mythological themes and constructs in order to draw conclusions
which retain their vitality outside the world of myth. This should
not be surprising, since myth is used frequently as an instrument or
tool for reflection throughout the Old Testament, beginning with the
Primeval History in Genesis 1–11. It would, on the contrary, be surprising if Israel's sages denied themselves this mode of reflection.
The authors of Proverbs introduce mythological motifs at many
points. They speak of the tree of life (11: 30), the fountain of life
(13: 14), Wisdom's house with its seven pillars (7: 6, 8; 9: 1). The
poem in chapter 8 is no more than an extension of this usage.

In spite of the uncertainty about Wisdom as artificer, the sense is
clearly that she presides over creation with God. To that extent we
have moved beyond the perspective of Job 28 in which the search
for her traces in nature proves to be unsuccessful. The point is made
more clearly in a related fragment (Prov. 3: 19–20):

> Yahweh by wisdom founded the earth;
> by understanding he established the heavens;
> by his knowledge the deeps broke open,
> and the clouds drop down the dew.

Wisdom, then, existed before everything else. Though created, her
relationship with God is unique. She was with him in creation and
in some way presided over it or co-operated with God in it. At the

same time, her relation to the created order remains to be spelled out. We shall go on to see that, in spelling it out, both Jews and Christians elaborated some of their most central theological affirmations.

Ecclesiasticus 24: 1–29: Torah assimilated to Wisdom

Ecclesiasticus (Ben Sira) is more of a book in the modern sense of the word than any of the compositions we have seen so far. We know the author's name from the epilogue to the original work (50: 27–9) and from the prologue to the Greek translation made by his grandson in Egypt some time after 132 BCE. The author, a scribe and teacher called Jesus but more commonly known by his patronym Ben Sira, also introduces occasional autobiographical allusions from which we gather that he was getting on in years (8: 6), that he had knocked about the world quite a bit (34: 9–12) and that, at the time of writing, he conducted a school or academy, presumably in Jerusalem (51: 23). The date of composition can also be established with a fair degree of accuracy. His historical survey ends with Simon II who was high priest at the time of the Seleucid conquest of Palestine (200–198 BCE), and there is no allusion to the usurpation of the high priesthood by Jason at the beginning of the reign of Antiochus IV about a quarter of a century later. He wrote therefore about 180 BCE, not long before the acute phase of the crisis brought on by the Hellenistic party in Jerusalem and the policies of Antiochus IV.

The author's conservative viewpoint may be deduced from the fact that he wrote in Hebrew at a time when it was quite common for Jewish authors to seek a broader audience for their works by writing in Greek, the language of the dominant culture. The same conclusion is suggested by his tireless insistence on 'the fear of Yahweh' as the basic principle of conduct and his denunciation of the impious who had abandoned the law (41: 8–10). He also takes issue with contemporary Jewish teachers who, misled by current philosophical trends, were denying free will and divine providence (e.g. 15: 11–20; 16: 17–23). His students are put on their guard against the dangers of philosophical speculation divorced from piety (3: 21–4); and it is possible that here and elsewhere he has Qoheleth in mind. His support of the Oniads, the legitimate high priestly family, went hand in hand with a moderate nationalism expressed in his prayer for deliverance from foreign rule (36: 1–17). We can only speculate on where he would have stood during the crisis which broke over Jews in the homeland not much more than a decade after he wrote his book.

Ben Sira was evidently concerned to respond to the challenge posed by Greek culture, but he proposed to do it in his own way. This is already suggested by the prologue which identifies Israel's wisdom as the law, the prophets, and the other writings. For the author himself the law is only part, although the most important part, of the curriculum he teaches (39: 1–5). As much as he insists on the observance of the commandments, it is clear that the category which dominates his thinking is not the law but wisdom. The structure of the book points unequivocally in this direction, and is probably based on the Book of Proverbs. It begins with a paean of praise for wisdom (1: 1–10), concludes with an acrostic poem describing his own lifelong search for it (51: 13–30), and has for its centrepiece the great apostrophe of wisdom (24: 1–29), to which we will shortly turn. This means that the book may be read as a defence of Judaism, based on the argument that Israel has its own wisdom which is superior to that of the Greeks. Josephus will take the same line in his treatise *Against Apion* following what was, in effect, a major point of Jewish polemic in Late Antiquity.

The opening statement (1: 1–10) makes it clear at once that, unlike the sages of an earlier day, Ben Sira regards wisdom as belonging to the divine world and available to humankind only as a gift. There is, therefore, a close parallelism between wisdom and the Spirit and, correspondingly, between the one endowed with wisdom and the prophet. Hence the author can speak of himself being filled with the spirit of understanding (39: 6) and pouring out his teaching like prophecy (24: 33). Following Proverbs 8: 22–31, he represents wisdom as first of all created things and the principle which informs the created order:

> It is he [Yahweh] who created her;
> > he saw her, and took her measure,
> > he poured her out upon all his works. (1: 9)

This view of reality leads him to defend the goodness and order of a world created by means of divine wisdom, a point by no means obvious to many of his contemporaries. While his starting point is in the Creation narratives in Genesis 1–2 which he paraphrases in his own way (unlike the modern biblical scholar, he reads them as one and undivided), his concern is to account for evil without imputing it to the Creator. An interesting argument along this line is that, while all things must come from God, nothing can exist without its antithesis; evil, therefore, is a necessary part of the created order:

> Good is the opposite of evil,
>> and life the opposite of death;
>> so the sinner is the opposite of the godly.
> Look at all the works of the Most High;
>> they come in pairs, one the opposite of the other.
>
> (33: 14–15)
>
> All things come in pairs, one opposite the other,
>> and he has made nothing incomplete. (42: 24)

Whatever we may think of this argument, it shows the author attempting to restate traditional texts in a more universally comprehensible language. A quite different but equally interesting example would be his survey of the national history (44–9). Departing quite radically from the mainline historiographical tradition represented by the Chronicler, he presents it in the form of short biographies, in keeping with a type of biographical writing, lives of philosophers, for example, which was at that time beginning to come into its own.

The central statement of the book—literally, since it comes in the middle (ch. 24)—is the apostrophe of personified Wisdom delivered in the divine assembly. This passage represents a further step towards the conceptual integration of the teaching of the sages with a religion based on the law. We saw that Deuteronomy 4: 5–8 identifies law observance with the wisdom proper to Israel. Ben Sira takes it a step further in identifying personified wisdom (*hokmah*) with law (*torah*). Wisdom, then, narrates in the assembly of the Most High how she proceeded from the mouth of God at the beginning of time, before anything was created; how she came down from her throne on a pillar of cloud to wander through the world in search of a resting place; and how the search ended when she came to rest in the sanctuary of the 'beloved city', Jerusalem (Ecclus. 24: 1–12):

> Then the Creator of all things gave me a command,
>   and my Creator chose the place for my tent.
> He said, 'make your dwelling in Jacob,
>   and in Israel receive your inheritance' . . .
> In the holy tent I ministered before him,
>   and so I was established in Zion.
> Thus, in the beloved city he gave me a resting place,
>   and in Jerusalem was my domain.
> I took root in an honored people,
>   in the portion of Yahweh, his heritage. (24: 8–12)

We see that, unlike the author of Proverbs 8: 22–31, Ben Sira draws freely on the historical and cultic traditions of his people. But here, too, it seems, Wisdom is modelled on a goddess who, in the context of that time, must have been none other than the Egyptian goddess Isis, or perhaps a Syro-Palestinian counterpart such as Astarte. The cult of Isis was very popular throughout the Ptolemaic empire, and remained so for long afterwards. The account of the epiphany of Isis to Lucius and his subsequent transformation, in book XI of the *Metamorphoses* of Apuleius of Madaura (2nd century CE), conveys a good impression of the fervour and enthusiasm inspired by this cult. Texts are extant in which Isis declares her praises and titles in the first person, describes how she presided over Creation as the eldest daughter of Re, identified with Chronos, and how she came down from her heavenly abode to search throughout the world for a place in which to establish her cult.

In one of these aretalogies, as they are called, originally written on a column in Memphis, she lists her titles and speaks of her role in Creation:

> I divided the earth from the heaven;
> I showed the path of the stars;
> I ordered the course of the sun and moon.

She was also known by the title 'lawgiver' and was identified by her theologians with Maat, principle of both cosmic and social order. In this capacity she proclaimed laws for humanity, maintained justice and righteousness, and sustained the social order. It seems that Ben Sira was familiar with these liturgical Isis texts and made use of them in his portrait of Wisdom. We can anticipate and say that his purpose in presenting an indigenized form of the Isis aretalogy was to claim for Torah a universal significance, and in so doing answer the charges of particularism and obscurantism that were in the air at the time of writing.

To return to our reading of the poem: The rustic imagery in which Wisdom goes on to describe herself (24: 13–22), and the erotic undertones of the invitation she sends out to her protégés (eating, drinking, honey and the honeycomb, and the like), bring to mind the courtly 'conceits' of the Canticle and fill out the sparer language in which the author of Proverbs 8: 22–31 described the Woman called Wisdom. Both provide interesting examples of intellectual and moral passion expressed in the language of physical desire.

The really novel element in Ben Sira's poem comes in the second part (vv.23–34) in which he identifies this pre-existent Wisdom with Torah:

> All this is the book of the covenant of the Most
>   High God,
>   the law that Moses commanded us
>   as an inheritance for the congregations of Jacob.
>
> (24: 23)

The identification will seem the more natural when it is recalled that Isis (Maat) promulgated laws, presided over the administration of justice, and maintained cosmic and social order. The law of Moses is therefore the supramundane principle of order as it has been made available to Israel. The manner in which Israel received this law is expressed in a kind of poetic midrash on the four rivers of Eden in Genesis 2: 10–14. It will be observed that Ben Sira brings the number up to six by adding the Jordan and the Nile:

> It overflows, like the Pishon, with wisdom,
>   and like the Tigris at the time of the first fruits.
> It runs over, like the Euphrates, with understanding,
>   and like the Jordan at harvest time.
> It pours forth instruction like the Nile,
>   like the Gihon at the time of vintage.

> The first man did not know wisdom fully,
>   nor will the last one fathom her.
> For her thoughts are more abundant than the sea,
>   and her counsel deeper than the great abyss.
>
>   (24: 25–9)

Drawing out the same metaphor, he sees himself as sage and instructor in the law, drawing water from this inexhaustible source to irrigate his own plot, namely, his school, becoming in the process a source of life and growth for others. It would be difficult to find a better metaphor for the tradition of Torah learning which Ben Sira inherited and passed on: a mighty river with tributaries and canals, bringing life to the land through which it passes.

While these speculations about wisdom and law were going on in academic and intellectual circles, they were not without effect on worship and piety. Psalms, including the longest in the collection, Psalm 119, often speak of the law as life-giving. The tone is set in Psalm 1, intended as a preface to the book, in which Ben Sira's metaphor is applied to the faithful who meditate on the law day and night:

> They are like trees
>   planted by streams of water,
> which yield their fruit in its season,
>   and their leaves do not wither.

The division of the 150 psalms into five books, though of uncertain date, also underlines the connection between law and worship, since it is clearly modelled on the five books of the Pentateuch. Even a rapid glance at the Jewish prayer book (the *siddur*) will suffice to show that, in the day-to-day practice of religion, piety and Torah study remained intimately related.

The Wisdom of Solomon: towards a new synthesis

The different strands of reflection and speculation woven by the sages whose compositions we have been discussing cannot easily be brought together into a cohesive philosophy or theology. We have seen some steps made in that direction, most recently by subsuming

proverbial and instructional material under the rubric of the unify-
ing concepts of wisdom and law. By the time of Ben Sira, Jewish
intellectuals in such major centres as Alexandria and Jerusalem were
beginning to reformulate Torah-religion as a philosophy. We know
some of their names, but their works have survived, if at all, only in
fragments. Ben Sira himself was no great philosopher, though he
attempted in his own way to respond to the challenge of the
Hellenistic 'enlightenment'. His identification of law with wisdom
influenced several writers whose works have survived from the two
centuries or so following.

One of these writers was the author of a short work listed in the
Apocrypha under the name of Baruch (second or first century BCE).
It purports to come from the hand of Jeremiah's amanuensis of that
name, but was in fact written by an anonymous Jew living at the time
of the Hasmonean principate. It contains a poem, of no great originality, describing wisdom as unknown to the nations of the world,
even those famous for wisdom, such as the Edomites, and undis-
covered throughout the course of history prior to the appearance of
Israel on the scene (3: 9—4: 4). This wisdom, with God from the
beginning, came down to earth and lived among humanity in the
guise of the Torah:

> She is the book of the covenant of God,
>   and the law that endures for ever.
> All who hold fast to her will live,
>   and those who forsake her will die.   (4: 1)

While the influence of Ben Sira will be noticed at once, the pattern
of pre-existence, descent, embodiment in Torah is clearly expressed.
Based on a mythic template, this pattern will in due course provide
early Christianity with a conceptual model for expressing its convictions about the identity and mission of Jesus.

The nature and role of wisdom are elaborated in a much more
ambitious way, and at much greater length, in a work written about
a century later for Greek-speaking Jews and interested Gentiles living in Egypt. Following the example of Proverbs, Ecclesiastes, and
the Canticle, the author locates his work within the sapiential tradition by donning the mantle of Solomon; hence the title The Wisdom
of Solomon which the book now bears. The first part consists of two

lengthy discourses of Solomon to his fellow-rulers (chs. 1–5 and 6–9). The first of these contrasts the fate of the impious, who justify their conduct by appealing to the Epicurean doctrine of fate, with that of the faithful whom they persecute and put to death. A decisive point in the author's apology for the life of observance, and a new one as far as we know, is the Platonic doctrine of the immortality of the soul, by virtue of which the righteous are vindicated and their death is seen as entrance into a blessed eternity:

> The souls of the righteous are in the hands of God,
> and no torment will ever touch them.
> In the eyes of the foolish they seemed to have died,
> and their departure was thought to be a disaster,
> and their going from us to be their destruction;
> but they are at peace. (3: 1–3)

The second of the discourses (chs. 6–9), in which the writer for the first time identifies himself with Solomon, tells how he acquired wisdom in answer to prayer. After listing the twenty-one attributes of wisdom, based apparently on a well-known Stoic hymn to Zeus, he goes on to state how it proceeds from God as a spiritual essence, and how it passes into the souls of those disposed to receive it. The last part of the book (chs. 10–19) deals with the role of wisdom in history, and especially the history of Israel, from Creation to the exodus. It includes a lengthy diatribe against the stupidity of idolatry, singling out as the most stupid kind of all the Egyptian worship of animals (theriolatry)—a point of obvious relevance to readers living in Egypt.

While most commentators do not seem to have been greatly impressed by The Wisdom of Solomon as a philosophical work, it can be argued that the attempt to place the Jewish religion within a broad philosophical context intelligible to educated contemporaries is, in some respects, remarkably innovative. Note, for example, how, in spite of his spirited defence of Jewish martyrs (whether in Judah or Egypt cannot be determined), and in spite of his detestation of idolatry, the author seldom alludes to the law except in passing (2: 12; 6: 4; 16: 6). He does not even mention it when he comes to speak of Moses' leadership of the Israelites in the wilderness (10: 15—11: 14), and Moses himself is a prophet rather than a lawgiver (11: 1).

He does speak of *wisdom's* laws in a passage in which traditional and non-traditional themes are brought together elegantly in the rhetorical figure of speech called sorites:

> The beginning of wisdom is the most sincere desire for
>   instruction,
> and concern for instruction is love of her,
> and love of her is the keeping of her laws,
> and giving heed to her laws is assurance of immortality,
> and immortality brings one near to God;
> so the desire for wisdom leads to a kingdom.   (6: 17–20)

This 'step' or 'stairs' form of argument, dear to Stoic preachers and familiar to Paul (e.g. Rom. 5: 3–5), provides an interesting example of theological restatement. The laws in question, wisdom's laws, certainly include the biblical laws, as the allusion to Deuteronomy 11: 1 makes clear: 'You shall love Yahweh your God, and keep his . . . commandments always.' But they are put within a broader context by being derived from wisdom as cosmic principle. In keeping with this perspective, the author's ethic is not based exclusively on the biblical laws. Much of it has been taken over from other sources, especially Stoic ethics, e.g. the cardinal virtues of self-control, prudence, justice, and courage (8: 7).

A further implication is that observance of Israel's law, far from being a petty, provincial affair, is Israel's way of being true to the God-bestowed order and harmony of the world. Like the world-soul of the Stoics, the wisdom of which the author speaks 'reaches mightily from one end of the earth to the other, ordering all things well' (8: 1). Following Ben Sira, he portrays wisdom as privy to divine knowledge and co-artificer of the created world (8: 4). She is therefore the source not only of the laws but also of the encyclopaedic knowledge attributed by the tradition to Solomon (7: 15–22). Her relationship to the divine world is expressed in an accumulation of metaphors:

> For she is a breath of the power of God,
> and a pure emanation of the glory of the Almighty;
> therefore nothing defiled gains entrance into her.
> For she is a reflection of eternal light,
> a spotless mirror of the working of God,
> an image of his goodness.   (7: 25–6)

This kind of language is reminiscent of Greek philosophical teaching on the mind (*nous*) or the active principle of the world (*logos*). It will make a significant contribution to early Christian theology, especially the doctrine of the Holy Spirit and Christology.

In the older wisdom, ethical instruction provided the link between cosmic order and the life of the individual. Wisdom stood for a certain quality of life attainable by the application of reason and the expenditure of effort. The readings so far in this chapter will have shown how different the situation was for teachers of a later time for whom wisdom belonged to the divine world and was attainable only as a gift of God. Following their lead, the author of the Wisdom of Solomon takes off from the biblical text about Solomon's prayer for wisdom (1 Kgs. 3, where he speaks of him achieving union with wisdom through searching and praying (7: 7; 9: 1–18). He believes that there is an innate bond between the human soul and this wisdom of divine origin. Souls are created immortal, since they are in the image of the immortal God; only at a later point did death come on the scene through the devil in the guise of a tempting serpent:

> God created us for incorruption,
> and made us in the image of his own eternity,
> but through the devil's envy death entered the world,
> and those who belong to his company experience it.
>
> (2: 23–4)

A good example, this, of the author's biblical interpretation. Unlike the critical biblical scholar, he reads Genesis 1–3 as one text, relating the creation of humanity in God's image in chapter 1 to the Garden of Eden story. He also brings his own philosophical hermeneutic to bear on the biblical text. Following Plato, he holds that the soul existed as a spiritual essence before entering into a perishable body (8: 19–20; 9: 15). The possession of wisdom is the pledge that the original integrity of the human person will be restored (6: 17–20; 8: 13, 17).

Wisdom also is a spiritual entity since she is intimately associated or even identical with the Spirit of God:

> Who has learned your counsel,
> unless you have given wisdom
> and sent yout holy spirit from on high? (9: 17)

This 'spirit of wisdom' (7: 7) enters the souls of those disposed to receive it, bringing with it what Christians will call 'the gifts of the Spirit':

> In every generation she passes into holy souls
> and makes them friends of God and prophets;
> for God loves nothing so much as the person who lives
>   with wisdom. (7: 27–8)

This view of wisdom as the source of the morally good life, what we might call anthropological wisdom, is also found in the works of the Jewish philosopher Philo of Alexandria (*c*.20 BCE–50 CE). While there seem to be no certain indications that Philo depended on the Wisdom of Solomon, a circumstance which complicates the task of dating the latter work, it is clear that Alexandria, one of the three great cities of the Roman empire together with Rome itself and Antioch, was one of the principal Jewish intellectual centres where this work of philosophical and theological synthesis was going on. It was there that the Scriptures were translated into Greek, that Ben Sira's book was translated, and that, in all probability, the Wisdom of Solomon was composed. After Philo, and greatly influenced by him, there emerged in Alexandria one of the most influential of Christian theological schools represented by Clement and Origen.

In the last section of The Wisdom of Solomon (chs. 10–19) the author introduces wisdom under a different aspect, i.e., as the active principle in sacred history. Something of this can be detected in Baruch, but the author of Wisdom takes in the entire span of time from Creation to the exodus, using wisdom as a principle of interpretation or reinterpretation. His method is quite different from the allegorical exegesis of Philo and early Christian writers; more like a specialized form of haggadic midrash then being practised by Jewish exegetes. But the author's very specific intent of 'sapientializing' biblical history results in a kind of treatise which is really *sui generis*. It is also dictated by the polemical needs of the situation in which he was writing. Hence his emphasis on the Egyptian phase of Israel's history and his taking a quite disproportionate amount of space to refute and ridicule idolatry, especially the kind practised in Egypt at that time.

The Wisdom of Solomon is not highly regarded as a philosophical work; in fact, it is not generally regarded as a philosophical work at all, and is not even mentioned in the standard histories of philosophy. One suspects that this is due less to its intrinsic merits or demerits as to the fact that it is too philosophical for biblical scholars and too biblical for philosophers. One would think, in any case, that the concern with wisdom as the source of the good life, a life worthy of God, should not in itself disqualify it as a philosophical work, for the same is true of most ancient philosophy. Unlike his modern academic counterpart, the ancient Greek philosopher—the Stoic, for example—saw his (less commonly her) vocation as a matter of living as well as understanding. The gap between the Jewish and the Greek concern with wisdom was not, then, as wide as we might be inclined to think.

Apocalyptic wisdom

Using a selection of the extant texts both in the biblical canon and outside, we have traced one line of development in the intellectual history of early Judaism during the last two or three centuries of the Second Commonwealth. The presence in the third part of the canon, the Writings, of Daniel, a quite different kind of book, points us to another direction taken by sagedom and scribalism, and one no less important for the future.

Daniel is an apocalypse, meaning that it treats of mysteries, concerned primarily with the course of the future and the supramundane world, as revealed by God to chosen intermediaries. The additions to Daniel in the Septuagint (the Prayer of Azariah, the Song of the Three Youths, Susanna, Bel and the Dragon) and fragments discovered at Qumran (especially the Prayer of Nabonidus which has affinities with Dan. 4) suggest that the biblical book was part of a larger Danielic cycle. No other apocalyptic treatises or tracts from the Graeco-Roman period were admitted into the canon, though we know that others were produced. While dates of composition are generally uncertain, these include writings attributed to Enoch, early Sybilline Oracles, and an Ezekiel apocryphon. Other works from roughly the same time-span contain apocalyptic elements, for example, the Testaments of the Twelve Patriarchs. The very extensive cycle dealing with Enoch, the sage of the archaic period who was taken up into heaven (Gen. 5: 18–24), contains sections older than Daniel, generally dated to 165 BCE. All of this material deals in one way or another with divinely imparted wisdom, but the point of view is significantly different from that of the texts discussed earlier in this chapter.

Debate on the origins of apocalyptic writing has, in recent years, tended to focus on the question of whether it developed from prophecy or wisdom. But this way of posing the issue is clearly unsatisfactory, especially if it gives the impression that we are dealing with three distinct and identifiable entities called prophecy, wisdom, and apocalyptic. It also tends to leave out of account the existence of apocalyptic outside Israel—in Babylon, Persia, and Egypt—during the Hellenistic period. In addition, scholars who make such claims often work with the development of ideas, leaving social situations out of account. If a study of the social co-ordinates of apocalyptic shows, for example, that certain situations and conditions tend to favour its emergence, it would not be confined to one period, and certainly not as the result of a gradual and inevitable transition from something preceding it. Not surprisingly, none the less, there are obvious points of contact between both prophecy and wisdom on the one hand and apocalyptic on the other.

One of these points of contact with prophecy is the claim advanced by the writers of apocalyptic tracts to interpret prophetic texts by means of divine inspiration. It is by virtue of this claim that the author of Daniel, who presents himself as a sage, is able to predict the course of future events. We have seen some examples of scribes and sages claiming for their writings an authority and inspiration in some sense prophetic. It is along this line that we trace a shift from inspired prophetic utterance ('thus says Yahweh') to an interpretative activity for which a comparable inspiration is claimed. This is one aspect of apocalyptic essential for understanding Daniel.

At first reading, the books appears to fall neatly into two parts: a series of court tales featuring Daniel and three companions (chs. 1–6); four visions dealing with the course of history and its imminent consummation (chs. 7–12). We may set it out as follows:

Court tales

1. Daniel and his friends at Nebuchadnezzar's court.

2. Nebuchadnezzar's dream.
3. The three youths in the fiery furnace.
4. Nebuchadnezzar's insanity.
5. Belshazzar's feast.
6. Daniel in the lions' den.

Visions

7. The four beasts and 'Son of Man'.
8. The ram and the male goat.
9. The seventy weeks of years.
10–12. The last days.

A complicating factor is that the work is bilingual, with Aramaic from 2: 4, where the Babylonian sages reply to the king, to 7: 28, the end of the first vision, and the rest of the book in Hebrew. This circumstance has led some scholars to suspect that the first vision (ch. 7) is meant to go with the court tales. There is, in fact, a rather close structural parallelism between the four beasts followed by the 'Son of Man' and Nebuchadnezzar's dream of the statue made of four different metals and the stone that broke it to pieces (ch. 2). Note, too, that the tales are not all of the same kind. Three (2, 4, 5) illustrate Daniel's wisdom as interpreter of divine mysteries, while the other three (1, 3, 6) are designed to show how God protects those who faithfully observe the laws, especially in the matter of false worship. The tales may have circulated independently of and earlier than the visions, though they are, in fact, rather well integrated with them. Also, their relevance to the situation of persecution out of which the visions were composed would have been immediately obvious.

These few introductory remarks must suffice for our present purpose, which is to enquire what, in this context, it means to be wise, and what is the origin of the wisdom with which the principal characters are endowed.

In the court tales the Jewish youths are 'skilful in all wisdom, endowed with knowledge, understanding and learning' (1: 4). Since they were put through a three-year curriculum in Babylonian science and letters, which would have included astronomy, omens, dream interpretation, and the like, their knowledge was clearly not confined to their own religious tradition. But there is concern to show that this kind of broad learning and the life of holiness can and must go together. Everything takes place in an atmosphere of observance, prayer, fasting, penitential exercises, visions, and communion with the supramundane world. Since the book was written in and for the pietist groups which opposed Antiochus IV and his Jewish collaborators, we may see in this portrayal of the main characters a profile of the sectarian and 'hasidic' ideal. It also seems likely that Daniel himself, who is carefully distinguished from his colleagues, stands for the leadership of the group. His distinctive competence is, at any rate, emphasized right from the start:

> To these four young men God gave knowledge and skill in every aspect of literature and wisdom; Daniel also had insight into all visions and dreams. (1: 17)

As we read on, we note that during the crisis precipitated by the mad tyrant's decision to exterminate the sages, all the youths prayed, but the mystery was revealed only to Daniel in a vision, allowing him to interpret the dreams about the statue (2: 17–45) and the great tree (4: 19–27). During the reign of Belshazzar, mistakenly identified as Nebuchadnezzar's son by the author, Daniel was able to interpret the writing on the wall by virtue of his 'excellent spirit, knowledge, and understanding to interpret dreams, explain riddles, and solve problems' (5: 12). In the second part of the book Daniel alone appears, and it is he who has the visions in which the course of history and its imminent consummation are foreseen. If the leaders of the sect from which the book comes are the ones referred to in it as 'the wise' or, more precisely, 'teachers' (Hebrew *maskilim*, literally, those who impart wisdom; 11: 33, 35; 12: 3, 10), it would be natural to find them exemplified in the profile of the principal protagonist of the book.

The point was made that, unlike the prophet, the apocalyptic seer does not ascribe supramundane authority to his message in his own person. The claim is, rather, that he has received a revelation from one of the sages of the past, generally the distant past. We thus have apocalyptic books under the name of Noah, Enoch, and even Adam. Daniel is somewhat different, since the author is represented as living during the Neo-Babylonian and early Persian periods. A heroic and wise figure bearing the name Danel or Daniel is featured in one of the Late Bronze Age epics from Ugarit-Ras Shamra and is mentioned in Ezekiel (28: 3, cf. 14: 14). In The Book of Jubilees, a sectarian composition from the second century BCE, a Danel is the father-in-law of Enoch, and is described as 'first among those who learned writing, knowledge and wisdom' (4: 20). It may be that this tradition about Danel–Daniel was transferred from the archaic period to the time of the exile because of the way the author of the book wished to narrate the course of history, depicting Antiochus IV Epiphanes under the guise of the Babylonian tyrant Nebuchadnezzar. The time of the exile provided a point of departure for a historical continuum leading up to and beyond the dark days through which Jews in the Seleucid realm were passing at the time of writing.

If it is accepted that Daniel and his companions stand for the members of the pietistic sect from which the book comes, it should be possible to find clues to the theory and practice of interpretation which was one of its most important activities. The 'text' to be interpreted, we might say, decoded, can be a written text—mysterious words appearing on a wall (5: 5–9), a Book of Truth stored in heaven (10: 21), in one case a biblical text, from the prophet Jeremiah (9: 2). But it can also be a dream or a vision, and not necessarily the dream or vision of the interpreter. The important thing is that, with the obvious exception of the Book of Truth, the real meaning, unknown to the original author of the 'text', is revealed *for the first time* to the inspired interpreter. We find the same kind of procedure in early Christianity and in the Qumran sect. A commentary on the prophet Habakkuk, discovered in the first Qumran cave (1QpHab), operates on the same assumption as Daniel:

God told Habakkuk to write down what would come upon the last generation; but he did not reveal to him the consummation of the age. And when he [Habakkuk] said, 'so that he may run who reads it' (2: 2), its interpretation refers to the Teacher of Righteousness to whom God made known all the secrets of the words of his servants the prophets.

(7: 1–5)

Something of the same procedure can be seen in Daniel: here is the dream; this is its interpretation (*pesher*). In Daniel, as at Qumran, the text is interpreted atomistically, in the sense that each item in the dream, vision, or written text has its own specific referent. Each part of the great statue, for example, corresponds to a specific kingdom and phase of history. In the vision of the four beasts, the ten horns on the fourth are the rulers who followed Alexander and the little horn with the big mouth is Antiochus Epiphanes, and so on. We note, too, that the interpretative process often takes place during or shortly after a visionary experience; and a further complication is that the vision itself is sometimes explained by a heavenly intermediate, generally Gabriel, who is a part of the vision.

We have looked into the matter of interpretation at some length since, for the group within which the book was written, the knowledge gained in this way is part of true wisdom. We might see it as combining traditional wisdom, which looks for enlightenment to the past, with the prophetic emphasis on present experience. It is important to add that these learned activities are linked with intense devotion to the ideal of observance and holiness. The visionary prepares for the revelation by fasting, prayer, and the confession of sin (2: 18; 9: 1–19; 10: 2–3). There is even a suggestion that it took place during a service of worship, as seems also to have been the case in early Christianity (e.g. Rev. 1: 10). The reception of the revelation called for praise and thanksgiving, as is apparent from the fragments of psalms scattered throughout Daniel. Here, too, comparison with the Qumran group would be useful, specifically with the Hymn Scroll from the first cave (*Hodayoth*, 1QH):

> These things I have come to know by your wisdom,
>   for you have uncovered my ears to wonderful mysteries.
>
> (1: 21)

To sum up: the apocalyptic milieu is quite different from that of the learned Ben Sira or the Wisdom of Solomon; it is, none the less, undoubtedly scribal and sapiential. We might view it as an attempt to pursue the 'hidden things' without surrounding the 'revealed things' which make up the sum total in Deuteronomy 29: 29. Speculation and mythic symbolism play a much larger part—even more so in the Enoch cycle which we have not included in our study. The fusion between learning and piety is much more intense, and the apocalyptic interpretation of history has become the touchstone of faith. The law is not identified with wisdom in the same way as in Ben Sira, but its strict observance, sharpened by the conviction of living in the last days, was basic to everything else.

Wisdom in transition: some further developments

While convenient and necessary, our practice of assigning texts to distinct categories as, for example, Apocrypha, Pseudepigrapha, Classical Judaism, can easily lead us to overlook continuities and similarities which need to be emphasized. 'Wisdom literature' did not, needless to say, come to an end with the closing of the canon or the end of the biblical period, and neither Judaism nor Christianity was hermetically sealed off from philosophical current in the Graeco-Roman world. In an earlier chapter we noted, in connection with Proverbs and Ecclesiastes, the practice of collecting the sayings of distinguished teachers in compilations bearing the title 'Sayings of the Wise'. This process continued, and is represented in Judaism, early Christianity (perhaps as early as the hypothetical Q document), and pagan philosophy. An example of this last would be the *Enchiridion* of Epictetus (*c*.50–120 CE), a brief manual of theoretical and applied Stoic ethics. An example of this sage's sayings would be:

Demand not that events should happen as you wish; but wish them to happen as they do happen, and you will get on well.

Much of the teaching contained in this work could have been appropriated without much alteration by both Jewish and Christian teachers.

The Mishnaic treatise *Pirke Aboth* provides a good illustration of the continuity of the sapiential tradition in early Judaism. In the first place, its attributions span the period from the second century BCE to the time of the compilation of the Mishnah towards the end of the second century CE. It takes up many of the themes of the older wisdom in Egypt and Israel:

All my days I grew up among the sages, and I have found nothing better for myself than silence. (1: 17)

Then there is the occasional enigmatic note, resembling the riddle, as in a saying attributed to the great Hillel:

> If I am not for myself, who is for me?
> And if I am for myself [alone], what am I?
> And if not now, when? (1: 14)

That there is no true wisdom without godly fear, without attention to the moral bases of life, is stated in lapidary fashion in one of the few extant sayings of the charismatic Hanina ben Dosa, first century CE:

> Those whose fear of sinning takes precedence over their
> wisdom, their wisdom endures;
> Those whose wisdom takes precedence over their fear of
> sinning, their wisdom does not endure.   (3: 11)

In general, these sayings attest to the great importance of the sage, the rabbi, as religious and intellectual leader in post-disaster Jewish communities. So, for example, R. Jose ben-Joezer says:

Let your home be a meeting place for the sages; be dusty with the dust of their feet, and thirstily drink up their words.   (1: 4)

There is nothing quite comparable to *Aboth* in early Christian literature, though some collections of moral aphorisms were in circulation by the end of the second century. One of these, known as the *Sentences of Sextus*, appears to have had the purpose of presenting the Christian life as a noble philosophy which, through wisdom, leads the soul to God. (It was as natural for people to consider Christianity a philosophical sect as it was for Josephus to call the Jewish sects 'philosophies'). Much of the content of the Sentences is not specifically Christian, and many of the sayings draw on the aphoristic wisdom of Proverbs and Ben Sira. From the earliest times the needs of Christian communities were met by exchange of correspondence and, in due course, manuals of discipline comparable in some respect to the Qumran rules began to appear. The first known to us is the *Didache* or *Teaching of the Twelve Apostles*, from the late first or early second century. Its first section (chs. 1–6) is in direct line of continuity with the old wisdom, and is probably Jewish in origin. The teacher addresses the neophyte as 'son', presents his moral lesson in the well-tried form of the Two Ways, and emphasizes strict control of the passions. Both the *Sentences* and the *Didache* illustrate the fact that the content of early Christian ethics had little to distinguish it from traditional and contemporary Jewish moral teaching.

Collections of sayings attributed to Jesus as sage were made by Gnostic Christians several centuries after his lifetime. One of these, the *Gospel of Thomas*, was discovered at Nag Hammadi in Egypt in 1945. Introduced as 'secret sayings of Jesus', it contains one hundred and fourteen sayings, proverbs, and parables several of which have parallels in the canonical gospels and some few of which, previously unknown, may go back to Jesus himself. They present him, for the most part, as dispensing esoteric wisdom to a circle of initiates:

Jesus said, 'He who will drink from my mouth will become like me. I too will become him, and the secrets will be revealed to him.'

Of the canonical gospels, Matthew is the one most interested in presenting Jesus as wise teacher. To this end, he organized the sayings of Jesus into five discourses, doubtless modelled on the five books of Moses. The first of these, the Sermon on the Mount (chs. 5–7), concludes with the familiar contrast between the wise person and the fool, the former who builds his life on rock, the latter on sand. The parable discourse, further along, concludes with what looks like the evangelist's signature:

Every scribe who has been trained for the kingdom of heaven is like a householder who brings out of his treasure what is new and what is old. (Matt. 13: 52)

While there is much more to the first gospel than that, it does seem to indicate the intent of placing the teaching of Jesus within the ongoing tradition of Israelite and Jewish wisdom.

The pre-existence of Torah is often commented on in the Midrash; indeed, Midrash Rabbah on Genesis opens with a passage identifying Torah as the blueprint God used in creating the world. For the most part, however, speculation about wisdom of the kind we have studied in Proverbs 8 and Ecclesiasticus 24 was confined to the mystical tradition. Speculation about the *shekinah*, the divine radiance, a feminine principle connected with the personified wisdom of the sages, served in the medieval mystical commentary called the *Zohar* (the Book of Splendour), and in the writings of the great sixteenth-century kabbalist Isaac Luria, as a kind of counter to the overwhelming masculinity of the deity. Early Christian speculation about the Holy Spirit also drew on the language of pre-existent wisdom, as a result of which some feminine elements came to penetrate Christian ideas about the godhead, though never in comfortable accord with orthodoxy. The personification of wisdom as co-agent with God in creation was developed in different ways by Philo and Christian theologians who took over from him the idea of the Logos (word) or Sophia (wisdom) as an emanation from God. In due course these topoi provided Origen, the great representative of the Alexandrian school in the third century, with categories in which to express the relationship of Christ to the Father.

Recent study of the New Testament has shown that this line of thought, based on wisdom speculation, emerged even earlier in the history of the Christian church. It can be detected in fragments of hymns embedded in the letters (e.g. Col. 1: 15–20) and it seems to have given rise to polemic in the Corinthian church as early as the fifth decade of the first century (1 Cor. 1–2). In the Sayings Source known to modern scholarship as Q (presumed to derive from the German *Quelle*, source), recoverable from Matthew and Luke, Jesus is represented not only as wise teacher but as personified Wisdom (e.g. Matt. 11: 16–19, 25–30; 12: 42; 23: 34–6, and parallels in Luke). Taking everything into account, there can be no doubt that the wisdom of Israel, especially in its later developments traced in the present chapter, provided a major impetus to the formation of Christian theology and ethics. At this point, however, we have moved beyond the scope of our enquiry.

SELECT BIBLIOGRAPHY

These suggestions for further reading are limited to English-language works, most of them fairly recent.

Works of Reference

The standard, and generally accessible, collection of non-biblical texts relevant to all aspects of our study is still J. B. Pritchard (ed.), *The Ancient Near East: An Anthology of Texts and Pictures* (Princeton, 1958), especially 133–72, legal texts, and 234–52, wisdom material; id., *The Ancient Near East*, ii. *A New Anthology of Texts and Pictures* (Princeton, 1975), especially 31–86, laws and treaties, and 136–67, sapiential and didactic texts. Also W. Beyerlin (ed.), *Near Eastern Religious Texts Relating to the Old Testament* (London, 1978) supplemented by W. G. Lambert, *Babylonian Wisdom Literature* (Oxford, 1960). For relevant Hebrew inscriptions see K. A. D. Smelik, *Writings from Ancient Israel* (Edinburgh, 1991) and for the Qumran texts G. Vermes, *The Dead Sea Scrolls in English* (London 1987, 3rd edn.). A good selection of religious texts from the Hellenistic period is available in F. C. Grant (ed.), *Hellenistic Religions* (Indianapolis, 1953); pseudepigraphal texts are translated in J. H. Charlesworth (ed.), *The Old Testament Pseudepigrapha* (2 vols.; Garden City, NY, 1983, 1985).

Wisdom in General

Standard surveys in J. L. Crenshaw, *Old Testament Wisdom: An Introduction* (London, 1982) and R. E. Murphy, *The Tree of Life: An Exploration of Biblical Wisdom Literature* (London, 1990); G. von Rad, *Wisdom in Israel* (London, 1972) is strongly theological in its approach; R. N. Whybray, *The Intellectual Tradition in the Old Testament* (Berlin, 1974); J. G. Gammie and L. G. Perdue (eds.), *The Sage in Israel and the Ancient Near East* (Winona Lake, Ind., 1990); L. G. Perdue *et al.* (eds.),

In Search of Wisdom (Louisville, Ky., 1993) together provide excellent coverage of most issues.

Wisdom: Special Topics and Commentaries

R. N. Whybray, *Wisdom in Proverbs* (London, 1965) and W. McKane, *Proverbs* (London, 1970) provide detailed commentary, and C. R. Fontaine, *Traditional Sayings in the Old Testament* (Sheffield, 1982) studies the proverb in general and proverbs elsewhere in the Hebrew Bible; M. Pope, *Job* (Garden City, NY, 1973); R. Gordis, *Koheleth: The Man and His World* (New York, 1951); E. Bickerman, *Four Strange Books of the Bible* (New York, 1967) has an original treatment of Jonah, Daniel, Ecclesiastes, and Esther; D. Winston, *The Wisdom of Solomon* (Garden City, NY, 1979); theodicy is the theme of J. L. Crenshaw, *A Whirlpool of Torment: Israelite Traditions of God as an Oppressive Presence* (Philadelphia, 1984); Marcia Falk, *Love Lyrics from the Bible* (Sheffield, 1982) provides a translation and literary study of the Song of Songs; M. Hengel, *Judaism and Hellenism* (London, 1974) provides a standard account of the Hellenistic period and the historical background of Ecclesiastes and Ben Sira, 115–53, supplemented with G. W. E. Nickelsburg, *Jewish Literature between the Bible and the Mishnah* (Philadelphia, 1981); id., *Faith and Piety in Early Judaism: Texts and Dcouments* (Philadelphia, 1983); M. Stone, *Scriptures, Sects and Visions: A Profile of Judaism from Ezra to the Jewish Revolts* (London, 1980) and J. J. Collins, *The Apocalyptic Imagination* (New York, 1987) cover Daniel, Enoch, and apocalyptic; R. L. Wilken (ed.), *Aspects of Wisdom in Judaism and Early Christianity* (Notre Dame, Ind., 1975) has essays on the place of wisdom in the gospel tradition, early Christian hymns, Paul, Philo, Midrash, and the Sentences of Sextus.

Law: Special Topics and Commentaries

A. Alt, 'The Origins of Israelite Law', *Essays on Old Testament History and Religion* (Oxford, 1966), 79–132, is still fundamental; up-to-date coverage of Pentateuchal criticism in D. A. Knight, 'The Pentateuch', D. A. Knight and G. M. Tucker (eds.), *The Hebrew Bible and its Modern Interpreters* (Chico, Calif., 1985), 263–96, and J. Blenkinsopp, *The*

Pentateuch (London, 1992); B. S. Childs, *Exodus: A Commentary* (London, 1974) especially 337–511 dealing with Sinai and the laws; A. D. H. Mayes, *Deuteronomy* (New Century Bible: London, 1979); R. J. Coggins, *The First and Second Books of the Chronicles and the Books of Ezra and Nehemiah* (Cambridge, 1976); J. Blenkinsopp, *Ezra–Nehemiah: A Commentary* (London, 1988); a good critical introduction is provided by D. Patrick, *Old Testament Law* (Atlanta, 1985) and H. J. Boecker, *Law and the Administration of Justice in the Old Testament and Ancient East* (Minneapolis, 1980); S. Greengus, 'Law', in D. N. Freedman (ed.), *The Anchor Bible Dictionary*, (6 vols.; New York, 1992), iv. 242–65; J. J. Stamm and M. E. Andrew, *The Ten Commandments in Recent Research* (London, 1967) is in need of updating but still essential reading; on the Priestly world-view see M. Douglas, *Purity and Danger* (London, 1966); P. J. Budd, 'Holiness and Cult', in R. E. Clements (ed.), *The World of Ancient Israel* (Cambridge, 1989), 275–98; J. G. Gammie, *Holiness in Israel* (Minneapolis, 1989); G. A. Anderson and S. M. Olyan (eds.), *Priesthood and Cult in Ancient Israel* (Sheffield, 1989).

INDEX OF PASSAGES CITED

NEW TESTAMENT

GENERAL INDEX